Programmed To Fail?

Discover How To Unlock The Solution To Your Problems And Become A Winner In The Game Of Life

Todd Wissler

Your Rights To This Information

© Copyright 2020 by Todd Wissler. All Rights Reserved.

The information in this book may not be sold or any parts of it copied or reproduced in any form without prior written approval of the Author.

Unauthorized duplication will result in appropriate legal action.

Legal Notice and Disclaimer:

This book is for informational purposes only.

The views expressed herein are those of the author who assumes no responsibility for any errors, omissions or interpretation of the subject matter. This information isn't intended to be a source of financial advice and it is recommended that you seek competent professional advice before engaging in any business activities.

The author accepts no responsibility for the use or misuse of this book, or for any financial loss sustained by anyone as a result of using this information.

While every effort has been made to ensure the reliability of the information presented in this book, it is based on our own experience and the liability from the use of the information is the sole responsibility of the reader.

No guarantees or claims as to the financial gains that might be made from reading this information have been given.

As at the time of writing the resources mentioned in this book have been accurately depicted in view of the author's own personal experience.

"This book is a GREAT WORK...an easy to read, practical and user-friendly guide to living a more happy and fulfilled life. It looks at many meaningful questions and gives valuable answers. I like that the author walks the talk, giving tangible examples of his own experiences. Everyone should have a copy on the shelf."

~ Dellaina Hascha - Teacher, Channel, Visionary Therapist and contributing author in the best selling series "*Adventures In Manifesting*". Diamond Harbour, New Zealand.
www.almora.nz

"If your life has been a struggle and you've tried The Law of Attraction, Mind Power, Positive Thinking, Self Hypnosis, learning how to set and achieve goals or any other modality that worked for a while then stopped, this book will help you understand what the other steps are missing."

~ Christine Breese, PhD., founder of The University Of Metaphysical Sciences in Arcata, CA.
www.metaphysicsuniversity.com

Introduction

So how's your life going? Great guns? Setting the world on fire at your job, working your way up the corporate ladder? Or you have your own business that keeps growing every year? You usually get what you want most of the time having more successes than failures? You have a great personal life with a great family and a lot of friends? You're able to get away and enjoy yourself with fun time every so often, can afford super vacations every year? You're a pretty happy person? You're living in your dream house? It's A Wonderful Life? That's beautiful. I'm real happy for you.

Or has your life been just the opposite? You can't get anything of a major importance you want...or when you do something always happens that causes you to NOT have it shortly thereafter? You're struggling with money even while working a full time job most of your adult life, even in an industry that pays fairly well...never being able to achieve your big goals, failing in love? It seems bad luck follows you? Your life is in constant turmoil? You see yourself as a loser?

No one thinks they're a loser because it's a cool or fun or hip way to view themselves. But a number of years goes by and some people see their lives are falling apart. They try a self improvement method and their lives start to improve for a few months, then it all stops working. Then they really start to think of themselves as a loser and their lives get worse. They feel trapped and start to believe there's no way out, that they can't do anything about it.

If the second example is your life story then you've found the right book because if you are "Programmed To Fail" for the same reason I was you're among a special group.

For Whom This Book Was Written

This book is for four types of people:

1. The first group are those who are victims of what I have named *"The Unwritten Universal Law."*

Spiritual Laws Of The Universe

I've read articles that claim there are 12 Universal Laws, other articles claim there are 33, another article says there are 8.

These are Laws that govern the Universe. They're called Laws because they can't be changed, and they effect everyone and everything in the Universe the same way.

Among them are "The Law of Divine Oneness" which says EVERYTHING in the Universe is interconnected. There's "The Law of Vibration"...every particle in the Universe is always on the move carrying and emitting energy. Then there's "The Law of Polarity" which says everything in the Universe has an equal opposite.

The most commonly known Law is "The Law of Attraction" which says "like attracts like." If you are a positive person giving off positive "vibes", have a positive personality and everything about you is positive including most if not all of your thoughts, then you attract positive things into your life provided by the Universe.

But if you're full of negativity having continual negative thoughts, you're pessimistic about yourself, life, people and the world, The Law works the same way. You then attract negative, pessimistic things into your life... again given to you by the Universe.

The Law of Attraction gurus teach that if you change your thoughts, your personality and everything else in your life to positive then you attract all the goodness the Universe has to offer. And therefore, if you practice The Law Of Attraction teachings you can attract from the Universe just about anything you want.

And those gurus are correct. I take no issue with what they teach...except for one thing. They've left out an important element that I call "The Missing Piece To The Self Improvement Puzzle".

And that is...in every article I've read – whether they list 8 Laws, or 12 or 33 – there's one I've never seen listed. So I'll take credit for identifying and naming it.

I've already told you I've named it...*"The Unwritten Universal Law."* It IS a law because it can't be changed and it applies to **EVERYONE** in the world the same way thereby meeting the criteria for a Law to be Universal. And here it is…

You will NEVER improve your life by learning "How To Use Your Mind Power", or by adopting Positive Thinking, or The Law Of Attraction, or Hypnosis or by "Improving Your Life By Improving Your Thoughts" or with ANY Self Improvement methods IF you're a victim of The Unwritten Universal Law...until you free yourself of it.

I go into it in much greater detail later on because it may not apply to you...but then again it might. If it does you will find that out if you practice what I show you. And I'll tell you what you have to do to free yourself from its grip.

2. The second group of people who will benefit from what I have to say are those who are NOT a victim of that Unwritten Law but are dealing with many of the obstacles I listed above for the first group... they have low self esteem because of their upbringing, been raised in households that had constant turmoil, abusive parents who were dealing their entire lives with their own negative emotional issues and psychologically and/or emotionally damaged their children... perhaps they were bullied a lot while growing up feeling isolated from the rest of the world, not given much encouragement from others in their sphere of influence, always attracting negative people into their lives, who see themselves as losers.

3. The third group I can help are those who have no passion for life, seem to be just going through the motions of living, see their job as "just a job", who ask the age old questions…

   "What's the meaning of life, why are we here if I can't enjoy it?"

   and need just a little spark, a little direction to turn their lives into something exciting...the way they wished it would be.

4. And another group who will find this book helpful are those who have had a pretty good life so far. They're already successful, can get what they want most of the time with enough hard work. But I can show them how to achieve greater greatness by taking their successes and good fortunes into the stratosphere.

But if you fit into any of the first three groups...

I Hear You...I Know You're Hurting

Trying to become successful by learning how to harness my Subconscious Mind Power showed me I was programmed to fail and was a born loser...a victim of that "*Unwritten Universal Law.*" But I was lucky to find out why I was and managed to free myself of it.

And that is a very common experience among many who have tried to use their Mind Power or other self improvement methods to improve their lives. It works for a while – for a few months they start to attain their goals and their lives start to get better and they think they have found "the answer"...or "the Holy Grail" – but then everything STOPS...and their lives revert back to the way they were before they started. And further attempts to improve their lives fail. Such was the case for me.

So this is one of the things that makes my message different. I'm not saying no one has mentioned this, but among the Mind Power and Self Improvement experts I have heard and read (and that's a lot of them) NONE has addressed this issue...at least not in any of their writings or talks I have read or heard. If they have mentioned this at some point and I missed it, then I apologize.

The experts are not purposely hiding this failure issue from you or are being dishonest in anyway, it's just that they haven't experienced what I have. They haven't lived my life.

If you are dealing with this issue your life will keep getting worse until you resolve it. And because of my life experience, I know what I'm talking about. I was programmed to fail.

My Story From The Beginning

It was almost as far back as I can remember...first grade. I had a feeling in the back of my mind. I was too young at the time to intellectualize and define it. But now I'm able to put it into words. It was a feeling that "something isn't right."

As I grew older and started to get desires for goals I wanted to accomplish, that "thing" was getting in the way of me succeeding at just about anything I set out to accomplish. And simple things such as not being able to acquire a lot of friends, not feeling free and easy around people, not being able to allow my mind to get caught up in the fantasy of reading a book of fiction, feeling frustrated so much about it that I avoided reading fiction books, avoided watching movies out of the fear I wouldn't get deeply involved in the stories, wouldn't be able to let my imagination "run away with it." As a kid I never saw "The Wizard Of Oz". And how many times had that been on TV back then? Once every year on network television.

As I continued to grow it was difficult connecting with people...and them with me. I started to play the trumpet in second grade...and I progressed pretty well, more than the average kid at my age. In third grade – just one year after starting – I played "My Country 'Tis Of Thee" from memory to start our class play.

Back in the classroom when it was over the teacher was telling us how proud she was that our play went well and said…

"and Todd was great. He didn't make any mistakes playing his trumpet."

But the progress stopped when I decided in 8th grade that I wanted to be a professional musician and started to immerse myself in it, practicing a lot, studying music theory, listening to as much music as I could. It felt that the more serious I became with my desire to become a great musician something was holding me back from progressing. A feeling of a grip around me was keeping me from being the musician and person I wanted to be, the way I felt deep down that I knew I could have been.

Jazz Me Blues

My number one desire playing trumpet was to be a great jazz musician. Improvisation is the essence of jazz. It allows musicians to make up music on the spot by improvising to the harmonic structure of the tune being played. It's spontaneous, played that way only once, never to be played that way again.

One day in tenth grade I told my music teacher I wanted to learn to improvise. We went to the music room during lunch period. He played piano while we played some blues. He stopped me a few times to make suggestions about which notes of the harmony to go after… "the color notes of the chords."

About the third time I tried, the music was flowing out of me. It was so spontaneous. My fingers pushed the valves of my trumpet on their own without me thinking about it as if they were on autopilot. And it sounded so good my teacher was saying…

"Yeah, yeah, yeah, that's it. That's it."

I can still remember how good it felt inside of me as the music gushed out...a feeling I had never experienced before. It was on a different plane from the feelings of love and sex.

But about 5 seconds later, it felt as if something put a big grip around my emotions, choking off my feelings. The music stopped flowing and those great feelings inside of me subsided.

What choked off my feelings after 5 seconds? What prevented me from building on those 5 seconds I experienced in my first attempt at improvising?

I continued to play trumpet for another ten years. I became a professional at age 16 and yearned to be a great jazz musician. But I never felt that spontaneous feeling or sounded as good again.

I had all the desire in the world to be a great musician. I devoted my life to it. I obviously had the talent and understanding of it because of how good I sounded for 5 seconds on my first effort at improvising. Why couldn't I have it? What STOPPED me from having it?

That grip I felt around me after 5 seconds was what I felt my entire life. Something was getting in the way of me living life. I felt I was just existing, not feeling the passion of living. I was determined to find out what it was.

The Mind Power Solution...For A While

When I got into my early twenties I became fascinated with the thought of programming one's mind to get what they wanted. I thought that was what I needed to begin my road to success...

"that will break through the blocks"...

or so I thought. I started to read books, the first one being "*Psycho Cybernetics*" by Maxwell Maltz.

A few years later I came across the book "*Three Magic Words*" by the late U.S. Andersen. It was on the same topic as this book…harnessing your Subconscious Mind Power. It was my introduction to the subject.

So I started to do what it said…saying affirmations every morning about how I was the greatest jazz musician who ever lived, that I was so spontaneous and creative, that I had the Power of God in me.

It started to work. While I didn't regain those great feelings I felt in my first attempt in high school, I did become better at improvisation.

It was summertime. I had the busiest summer of my musician career playing a lot of gigs. The musicians I worked with were saying things such as…

"Hey man, you must be practicing a lot.
You're sounding better and better."

I wasn't practicing more than usual. Mind Power was making me better and better.

I kept getting better for about two months and was so happy I thought I found the answer…simply program the mind for what you want. After all, that's what all the self improvement, Mind Power, Law of Attraction experts say, right?

But then for some unknown reason (unknown at the time), everything stopped. I wasn't spontaneous anymore, my improvising reverted back to the way it was before. I did more and more affirmations but they didn't work anymore. I was feeling that "grip" around me again. It STOPPED working and I felt I was back to "square one". Now I know why. I was a victim of... ***"The Unwritten Universal Law."***

I've come to learn that my story is not unique, that many people have applied Mind Power or other self improvement methods to improve their lives. And it worked for a while...then stopped. But why? Why would something that causes your life to get better work for a while then STOP? Something has to be getting in the way.

But Enough About Me

And now, *you* want to learn how to use your Mind Power to get the life you want, huh? You've read many accounts of people using theirs to attract things they desire and to build the life they want. And now you're ready to give it a try.

This book will teach you the process. But will it work? That depends on you.

And I'm not talking about the usual "stuff" such as…

"If you have the determination to make it work it will."
Or…
"If you have the desire to succeed and put to use what I teach you it will work."
Or…
"The only way this won't work is if you don't apply it."

I'm sure you've heard those things before. But that's not what I mean.

Just What Are You Getting At, Todd?

OK, OK. We'll get into that soon. But from the beginning you'll learn how to harness the Subconscious Mind Power you already have. We all were born with it. It's one of our birth rights. You just have to learn how to use it.

And once you do -- provided you're not a victim of that Unwritten Law – you'll be able to use it to get just about anything you want…success, wealth, your dream job, your soul mate, friends with the characteristics you want, curing and preventing disease, releasing fears and phobias, healing broken relationships by rewriting history…and more.

I'll even show you how to use your Mind Power to get…what you *don't* want. Hang in there for that one. You'll find it very helpful when you get to it.

But Why Listen To Me?

The Self Improvement industry is huge. One of its sub-niches – The Law Of Attraction – is one of the most searched topics on the internet right up there along with health, fitness and…uh…..shhhhh!!!....s-e-x.

The industry has Self Improvement authors everywhere in the media promoting their books. They're regular celebrities. You'll also see them on TV when your local PBS station holds its fund drives as the gurus give away their programs for you to make a huge donation to the station.

So why listen to what a nobody such as I has to offer when there are gazillions of Mind Power/Self Improvement/Self Empowerment/ Hypnosis/Law of Attraction messengers and messages out there? First of all I keep it very simple. Although I do introduce you to much greater concepts near the end so you can take your mind power to your greatest heights possible *if you want to*, there are no exercises you have to perform in the beginning to unleash your power. Just understanding how the subconscious works and how you program it as I show you is all you need to know. But it's up to you to apply it.

There are no journals or work books you have to use to keep tract of your progress, no audios to listen to while traveling to and from work or school.

So with what I show you, less is best. All you have to do is spend 15 to 20 minutes a day putting into practice what I show you. If you can't devote one quarter to one third of one hour a day creating the life you want, then this is not for you.

Another reason why you should listen to me is because my main message is different from what I've heard ANY guru say. This will work IF you're not a victim of...

"The Unwritten Universal Law"

Heard any experts say that? All of them say ANYONE can improve their life by improving their thoughts. But I will show you later that – *"EVERYONE CAN DO THIS"* – is not always true.

If you're a victim of that Unwritten Law you will NEVER improve your life no matter how many self improvement books you read (except this one, of course), no matter how many success seminars you attend, nor studying courses that teach you how to set and achieve goals...until you free yourself from the grips of that Law.

I know that first hand because I went through many of the self improvement methods out there, spent years in traditional therapy trying to overcome whatever it was that was holding me back, that had a grip around me that was keeping me from being all I knew I could have been, that had bad luck following me, kept me struggling with money... all to no avail. It wasn't until I became aware that I was a victim of "The Unwritten Universal Law" and worked to resolve it that I finally broke the chains that kept me failing, and in doing so my life finally improved.

Good News For You

This book will tell you everything you need to know to send your Subconscious Mind Power into the stratosphere. It will also let you know if you're dealing with the same failure issue I was and what you must do to resolve it so you can have the life of your dreams. And there's a 100 percent chance that those under the spell of the Unwritten Law don't even know it...until someone or something — some revelation — makes them aware of it.

Another reason I want you to listen to me is because I know that what I teach works…not because I studied it in college and earned a Ph.D., nor conducted years of scientific research in some lab or ivory tower. I've done something more credible than any of that. ***I've lived it!!!***

Because of my struggles I learned all this by doing it and shared it with others and have seen them get great results with it. So I know from my own experience what works for some…but not for others.

I'll give you insights into the human psyche so you can understand why you are struggling and learn how you can completely eliminate the subconscious programming that has caused your problems.

You'll also learn how you can help yourself and those close to you – spouse, children, relatives, friends – resolve psychological issues that are making your lives difficult WITHOUT having to spend years – and a lot of money – in therapy.

Plus, I'll show you why your Subconscious Mind isn't just yours...how your thoughts travel far and wide throughout the entire Universe for an eternity enabling you to call upon "The Universal Subconscious Mind" for extraordinary life results.

And I'll awaken you to the journey you're on and the world in which you're *really* living while you're not even aware of it. Upon realizing it, you'll be able to put your Mind Power on steroids.

Your One Source

I also teach you how the Subconscious Mind thinks so you can use it to fit any situation you want...to attract or change just about anything in order to make your life more fulfilling. You'll discover that the solution to just about any difficult life situation is right inside you.

You'll become an expert in the Subconscious Mind and human psyche. You won't have to buy one book to learn how to attract success, then another to break addictions, then another to get your dream job, then another to improve your self esteem, then another to cure yourself of disease, then another to learn about and master The Law Of Attraction or Self Hypnosis, etc., etc.

When you use your Mind Power to attract wealth, then use it to quit smoking, then use it to attract a soul mate and all the other things for which you can use it, your Subconscious Mind worked the same way. It was the same process for reaching each goal. The only thing that was different was the desire you were trying to attain...and the words you used to acquire it.

And I will never have to come out with my "New And Improved" book because what I show you is how the Subconscious Mind has worked since the beginning of time, is working now and will ALWAYS work.

So what I'm saying is – if I may say so myself – this is the only book you'll need to learn how to use your Subconscious Mind Power to create the life you want…or to discover why you keep failing when you've tried everything, and what you must do to end your struggles.

But don't stop learning from this. I encourage you to try other modalities that can take your Mind Power to even greater heights. I talk about some of them later on. You'll have a much greater understanding of them and will get better results from them once you learn these fundamentals of the Subconscious Mind. What this book shows you is just the start of your Subconscious Mind Power journey.

So now…I'd say it's time to get started, wouldn't you?

"DRUM ROLL, PLEASE!!!!"
RRRRRROOOOOLLLLL – BLOP, JING!

Ladies and Gentlemen, without further ado…here's to your success at getting the life you want…or to turning yourself from a born loser like I was to a winner in the game of life.

About The Author

Todd Wissler is not a Ph.D. in psychology or anything else. He did not conduct years of scientific research in some lab or Ivory Tower to discover what he has learned. He has done something more credible than that. He has LIVED IT! He is just an ordinary guy. But from what he has learned he was able to write this book without having to look up case studies or white papers online or at the local library. It's all based on his experiences.

By overcoming his life struggles he has mastered the discipline of Subconscious Mind Power and in doing so has discovered what he calls "The Missing Piece To The Self Improvement Puzzle", something that none of the established self improvement gurus talks about.

And that is...no one can improve their life if they are a victim of what he has termed *"The Unwritten Universal Law"* unless they resolve that issue first. Until they do, nothing will help them improve their lives, not The Law of Attraction, or Positive Thinking, or Hypnosis, or learning how to achieve goals, or not even years of traditional therapy.

You can learn more about Todd Wissler at his website…

www.SuccessExclusives.com

Contents

Part Three: Beyond The Earth Plane

PART 1

Start Your Engine Please

CHAPTER 2

The Conscious Or Subconscious – That Is The Question

First…congratulations on taking the initiative to putting your destiny into your own hands. When you come to realize the Mind Power you already have and learn how to harness it, you are definitely taking charge of your life.

Thank you so much for allowing me to help you in this endeavor. It's such a great feeling for me to be a source of enlightenment to you…to "show you the way" so to speak.

It's unfortunate that most people never come to know the power that they already possess…Subconscious Mind Power. And many people who become aware of this power by hearing of it from others or reading how others have attained great success by using their Power won't take the time to learn how to master theirs. Skepticism is a good thing but not when it keeps one from investigating a topic to see if it's something that can work for them.

Non-believers use their Mind Power without even knowing it. They use their gut instincts or "hunches" to help them make decisions all the time. It's their Mind Power speaking to them, but they never know it as such. They never come to see that it's their Mind Power working for them.

Everyone who has learned how to harness their Mind Power leads a happy and fulfilled life. Learning how to unleash that power can unlock your fullest potential giving you greater greatness, more joy and happiness, bringing wealth and abundance into your life, allowing you to prevent and cure disease.

I become so saddened when hearing about people struggling for years fighting diseases such as cancer, dragging their family and friends with them through the ordeal and finally succumbing. If they had only known about the healing power of their Subconscious Mind they could have avoided all that pain and suffering.

But you are different. You're among the select few who want to take the step, to learn how to unleash their almost unlimited Mind Power and bring it fully into their lives. For that, I salute you.

Using your Mind Power to get what you want is not a new idea, or a relatively new one. It's as old as the Universe itself. It's the engine behind "The Law of Attraction." What your mind focuses on is what you attract. It's one of the Laws of the Universe.

But unfortunately, many people use "The Law of Attraction" to bring bad things into their lives by worrying about things that could go wrong, worrying about lack of money, lack of luck, having low self esteem, seeing themselves as losers. Focus on those things by worrying about them and that's what you'll attract.

You limit yourself by your own limiting thoughts and beliefs about yourself and the power you inherently possess. When you learn to harness your Mind Power and take it to extreme levels as I teach you, you'll learn how nearly unlimited your potential is.

So...Which Mind Is It?

I've been talking about "Mind Power" but yet haven't answered what I posed at the beginning of this chapter.

We have a conscious mind and a subconscious mind. Which one would you say determines what our lives will be like? If it were the conscious mind, then wouldn't everyone be happy, with a great job, a beautiful home, a great family, friends, possessions, wealth, or at least enough money so life is not a struggle financially? Doesn't everyone *consciously* want those things?

Why do some people have them and others don't? Why do some people who have gone to college, work hard and are good people struggle through life, while some others have a pretty good life...even those who don't have a lot of education, maybe are even high school dropouts, don't seem to put a lot of effort into things, and may not appear to you to have much ambition?

Why do some people always seem to have bad luck following them with their lives in constant turmoil? You may know some of them. Perhaps your life is like that. And then…there are others who whatever they touch turns to gold.

No rational, sane person ever existed on this planet who *consciously* wanted to fail and struggle through life. So the correct answer is…it's what's in your *Subconscious Mind* that determines how your life will be.

What Makes You...You?

Your conscious mind has nothing to do with who you are as a person. That's the mind that houses your intelligence, knowledge you acquire over the years, and your cognitive tools you use to make decisions.

Why do successful people usually make the right decisions, while the unsuccessful ones usually make the wrong ones? They both use their conscious mind the same way...information in, then the analysis, and then the decision is chosen. What caused the result of that decision to be what the successful person wanted, but the opposite of what the unsuccessful one wanted?

Choosing which decisions to act upon (the eventual right or wrong one) and everything else that makes you unique -- your personality, desires, the foods you like, the music you listen to, the people you're attracted to, the sports you like or dislike, your destructive habits, the people and situations you attract, how lucky or unlucky you are, your successes and failures, the career you choose, even the state of your health (I could go on and on) -- come from your Subconscious Mind.

Is Determination Enough?

Now we can discuss what I was trying to get at in the Introduction... having this work depends on you.

You've probably heard the saying...

"*You can do anything you put your mind to.*"

But is that really true...for EVERYONE?

If you read self help books or attend success seminars that show you how to set goals and you spend each day trying to attain them and you eventually have a great life, it's true that it was your conscious effort, desire and determination to succeed that led you there. You...

"*put your mind to it.*"

But the bigger picture is...

THERE WAS NOTHING IN YOUR SUBCONSCIOUS THAT STOPPED YOU.

I'll explain this aspect later on.

In making claims to back up their Mind Power message you'll hear many gurus say something such as...

"*The one thing that's different between you and the very successful/ wealthy is that they have learned the secrets to using their Mind Power to get what they want.*"

I certainly haven't spoken to all very successful/wealthy people. But I can tell you that most of them have **not** taken the time to do what you have decided to do...learn how to harness their Mind Power. They didn't have to. Most of them are successful and wealthy simply because...

just as there are born losers in life, there are also born winners.

People who are successful are NOT programmed in their Subconscious Mind to fail. Even those who have had very unsuccessful earlier lives – many of them near bankruptcy – finally found something that clicked – a product or formula of some kind – and then they became a success. It just took some time of failing – trial and error – that made them more determined to hit it big. For them, determination was enough.

But for those who are programmed to fail for the same reason I was can ***NEVER*** improve their lives – no matter how much determination they have and how hard they try -- if they don't uncover and rid from their psyches the reason that's causing them to have such lousy lives. More on that coming up.

Power Of The Mind...But Which One?

You've heard experts say...

"*The mind is very powerful.*"

Perhaps without realizing it, the mind they're referring to is the Subconscious. It works differently than the conscious mind does. When you understand the differences and learn how the Subconscious Mind thinks and how to harness its power ***CORRECTLY*** – provided you're not a victim of...

"The Unwritten Universal Law"

it can give you just about anything you want...all those things I mentioned in the introduction...and more.

So why isn't everyone using their Subconscious Mind Power? Most people haven't been made aware of it. It's not taught in school or part of our mainstream culture as it is in some Eastern countries. Or for those who have been made aware of it and have tried to put it to work but failed to do so didn't learn how to properly use it. Or they've given up after trying just a few times believing it doesn't work.

Or it didn't work for another reason, perhaps the biggest reason it won't work which I reveal later on, the reason why millions of people – perhaps even you – are born losers.

And I should know. After all, I was a born loser myself.

On To New Horizons

I want you to change your thinking in several ways. When you think about Mind Power or hear people talk about it, know that it's the power that comes from your Subconscious Mind, not the conscious mind.

And get excited that you're going to learn how to tap into an almost unlimited reserve of power you never knew you had.

Think of how this is the beginning of a new venture for you…one that could just be the most important venture of your life. You're going to be among the select few who journey into the world of… "*the mysterious*"… having it come to light for you so you can take advantage of it.

As Albert Einstein said…

"*The most beautiful thing we can experience is the mysterious. It is the source of all true art and science.*"

There's a new world awaiting you...that of your Subconscious Mind. What you perceive and experience on the conscious level is just the tip of your awareness iceberg. You're going to be harnessing that huge reservoir of power that's beneath the surface waiting to be tapped… just sitting there waiting for you to call on it to help you have the life you want.

Or if you're "Programmed To Fail" as I was, get excited about the fact that you're going to learn two things: why you're struggling, and the one and **ONLY** thing you CAN and MUST do to change that.

CHAPTER 3

It *IS* What You Say

You may have heard the saying…

"It's not WHAT you say that counts, but HOW you say it."

That's true for political pundits, sports analysts and others who get paid big bucks to speak on TV during news round tables and sports pre and post game shows. Those experts are professional talkers. Everyday, mundane "speak" is not very intriguing to listen to at those times. So they get paid a lot of money for "HOW" they express their views.

But when it comes to Subconscious Mind Power, WHAT you say is equally important as HOW you say it.

Simply Stated

I can tell you in two sentences how to unleash your Subconscious Mind Power to get just about anything you want:

Trick The Subconscious Mind Into Believing You Already Have What You Want. Then It Will See It And Deliver It To You.

There are many ways to accomplish that. Saying affirmations is the granddaddy of them all and has been around the longest.

An affirmation is simply a statement you affirm to be true. If you say it enough and believe it, your Subconscious Mind will believe it and allow it to come into being (but...who or what delivers that desire to you? We'll get into that later because you don't need to know that now.)

Saying affirmations is the only method I have used so it will be the only one we'll be using throughout this book. One reason I like saying affirmations is you don't need any special equipment…no software, for example. You just use what you were created with. You can certainly investigate other methods once you've mastered this one.

So with that being said, this is all you need to know to put your Mind Power to work. I call these…

The 6 Keys That Unlock Your Subconscious Mind Power

The Subconscious Mind…

1. Only thinks in the present
2. Does not know the difference between what is real and what is imagined
3. Learns by repetition...over and over and over again
4. Only thinks in infinite or absolute terms
5. Works quicker at getting you what you want if when saying affirmations you feel the emotions you would feel if you had it
6. Your conscious mind is your logical, rational, analytical, judgmental mind. Your Subconscious Mind is your il-logical, ir-rational, non-analytical, non-judgmental mind

(To keep it short I'll refer to these as ***"T6KTUYSMP!"...***just kidding.)

And that's it. You don't have to know anything more about how the Subconscious Mind works for you to harness its power. Do I make it sound simple? That's because it is.

The Subconscious Mind is not some extremely complex instrument or organ as you'll hear other experts claim. It is complex if you don't know how it works. But you will know before you finish reading this book. You'll be an expert.

However, training it to deliver you what you want takes time and practice. Before we begin to talk about that, I'll expand on **The 6 Keys** to give you a deeper understanding of them.

From here on out I'll say "Your Power" when referring to Your Subconscious Mind Power.

Key #1 - The Subconscious Mind only thinks in the present

This is where the Positive Thinking message falls short...in two areas.

First, here's how the term is defined on a website:

"Positive thinking is a mental attitude in which you expect good and favorable results. In other words, positive thinking is the process of creating thoughts that create and transform energy into reality. A positive mind waits for happiness, health and a happy ending in any situation."

(from the website: *https://leadingpersonality.wordpress.com/2013/03/15/what-is-positive-thinking/*)

So why is that claim *almost* correct? Two things…the words in the first line… "*in which you EXPECT good and favorable results.*"

And in the third sentence: *"A positive mind WAITS for happiness, health and a happy ending in any situation."*

First of all, the Subconscious Mind only thinks in the PRESENT - NOT in the future or the past. When you EXPECT good and favorable results from Positive Thinking, you're *waiting* for them to result…in the future in which the Subconscious Mind does not think.

So when you want to get the results you're seeking through Mind Power or The Law Of Attraction or Self Hypnosis or whatever you want to call it since they're all pretty much the same thing -- you must change your thinking to that of *imagining* you have what you want NOW...not by waiting and expecting it to happen.

NOW, NOW, NOW! That's the only way the Subconscious Mind thinks. You have to act and feel as though you have what you want NOW or it will always stay out in the future.

Thank You So Much Dr. Peale, But...

It was Dr. Norman Vincent Peale who brought the issue to the forefront of human awareness in his legendary book, ***"The Power Of Positive Thinking."*** But he "almost got it right" as I'll explain as we go through this book.

Dr. Peale wrote...

"Your unconscious mind...[has a] power that turns wishes into realities when the wishes are strong enough."

Ahhhh, yyyyeah...that's "almost" totally correct. And I'll show you how to make those "wishes" strong enough later on.

But let's look at how to take the message of "Positive Thinking" to another level. Here are some examples of thinking positively:

"I'm going to be a successful businessman." "I'm going to be a great athlete." "I'm going to be a great actor." "I'm going to be a great musician." "I'm going to get a great job." "I'm going to beat this disease."

All of those statements are positive, correct? But why won't the Subconscious Mind deliver those desires to you if stated that way?

Because the statements are being made about something in the future, not in the present. It's like the carrot and stick. As time goes on, the carrot (your goal) will always stay out in front of you (in the future) without you ever catching up to it.

You have to go beyond Positive Thinking by taking it to the next level. This is how the statements should be said:

"I AM a successful businessman." "I AM a great athlete." "I AM a great actor." "I AM a great musician." "I HAVE a great job." "I HAVE beaten that disease."

Your Power: A Double-Edged Sword

Without realizing it, we all use our Subconscious Mind correctly when we think negatively about ourselves. If in striving to reach an important goal such as a career choice we hit some hurdles along the way and think we're never going to attain it and become very discouraged, we don't say…

"I'm GOING to be the most unsuccessful businessman." "I'm GOING to be the worst athlete of all time." "I'm GOING to be a lousy actor when I'm 25."

We say it this way…

"I AM the most unsuccessful businessman." "I AM the worst athlete." "I AM a lousy actor."

So we know how to think correctly when we get discouraged and think negatively about ourselves. Just do the same when you think positively and want to attain a goal...it's NOW, NOW, NOW, not that you're going to get it -- or be it -- in the future. You have it -- or are it -- NOW!

Key #2 -- The Subconscious Mind does not know the difference between what is real and what you imagine to be real

The Subconscious Mind controls all your bodily functions. Ask your doctor next time you see him/her. They learned that in medical school.

Why do we keep breathing when we're asleep (and awake for that matter)? Do you have to consciously think about breathing? When you get done eating, do you have to consciously think about turning on your digestive system? What keeps your heart and pulse beating? What keeps your organs functioning? Your Subconscious Mind does.

And It Does Much More

Have you ever gotten into a heated argument with someone...a friend or work colleague in which you're in each other's face yelling at one another? What happened to your heart rate and pulse? They sped up on their own, right? You didn't consciously cause them to. Your Subconscious Mind did.

Also, you may have been trembling some and your adrenaline was flowing. Your Subconscious Mind caused all of that as a way to inform you that you were in a potentially threatening situation so you could get in a defensive posture.

Let's say someone at work did or said something that made you very mad but you didn't confront them about it for whatever reason. But when you got home and were still mad you promised yourself you were going to confront them the next chance you had.

So you start to practice what you're going to tell them and you really get into it. You imagine you're in their face telling them off and pointing your finger at them and you practice it many times and feel angry while you're practicing and get angrier the more you practice.

What happened to your heart rate and pulse? They sped up just as they would if you were actually confronting the person, right? Did you tremble somewhat? Of course. Why did that happen?

Again, your Subconscious Mind caused it because it *believed* the confrontation was really happening. It saw it as happening. You were just imagining it. But your Subconscious Mind couldn't tell the difference.

And when you got done practicing, did you say…

"*Hey, where did he go? Wasn't he just here? Wasn't I just yelling at him a few seconds ago? I thought he was here and I was yelling at him, wasn't I?*"

No. You never once consciously thought that. You knew in your conscious mind that the confrontation wasn't happening, that you were only imagining it.

It didn't matter. Your Subconscious Mind saw it (because you were doing and saying it in the present), believed it was happening and responded accordingly.

One Mind – Two "Chambers"

See how your conscious mind can think independently of your Subconscious? We have just one mind…but it has two separate "compartments" so to speak that serve separate functions. What you think in the conscious mind is not always the same as what's in the

Subconscious. That's why people can see things in a person that the person cannot such as psychological nuances.

For example, a person may be belligerent to others without consciously noticing it. Others do however, and are repelled by it. Something in the person's Subconscious is bugging him/her of which they're not consciously aware.

But getting back to imagination…do you need another example to believe **Key #2**? Why are good actors able to cry "real tears" when they have to? They're only imagining the situation that causes them to cry. They're pretending the situation is happening and are imagining the feelings. The Subconscious Mind can't tell that it's an imagined experience and the tears flow.

So as you can see, imagination is very powerful. And what's great about it is when you imagine something you can have it any way you like. You can have green roses, red oceans, brown sunlight.

I remember reading about a study at a university in which researchers gathered three groups of students and had them shoot basketballs for half an hour. Their scores were recorded.

Then for one month, one group didn't practice, another group practiced shooting baskets for half an hour every day, while the third group spent half an hour each day only *imagining* they were practicing and sinking every shot.

A month later, the students shot baskets and the researchers recorded their scores. The group that didn't practice didn't improve, the group that practiced improved, while the students who only *imagined* they were practicing improved just one percentage point less than the group that had actually practiced.

Freezing...On The Sun?

With our current technology, it's impossible to land a spacecraft on the sun. Because of the intense heat, the ship would burn up long before it got there.

But you can imagine you're standing on the sun and that it's extremely cold. And if you imagined you were cold strongly enough that the Subconscious Mind believed it, you could even start to shiver and get goose bumps...***while you're standing on the sun!*** You could convince your Subconscious Mind you're on the sun and shivering because of the extremely cold temperature.

"*Standing on the sun and shivering from the cold.*"

That doesn't make logical sense, does it? But as you'll learn in a moment, the Subconscious Mind doesn't think logically.

Key #3 - The Subconscious Mind learns by repetition...over and over and over again

This is extremely important to remember when starting to develop Your Power. If you're learning a new skill such as playing a musical instrument, becoming an athlete, actor or artist, do you think you only have to practice a little to become proficient? You have to practice over and over and over again. The more you practice, the better you become and the easier it gets to execute the mechanics.

The same is true with the Subconscious Mind. In learning how to harness Your Power, you're learning a new skill and it also takes time to develop. That's why many people give up trying to harness their Power after several tries believing it doesn't work. It does...but it takes time. However, as with all other skills the more you use Your Power the easier it works.

Think of your Subconscious Mind as a muscle you've never exercised. If you decide you want a nice physique and start pumping iron for the first time in your life, you don't expect to look like Mr./Ms. Olympia after one or two workouts. It takes time for those muscles to grow and become stronger.

If you use Your Power to dissolve a cancerous tumor from your brain and you say just several times…

"The tumor in my brain has dissolved away"

and leave it at that, the tumor will not go away.

But if you say…

"The tumor in my brain has dissolved away"

over and over again for, let's say…20 minutes several times a day for a month…then you stand a very good chance of being cured (provided you don't spend time in between those 20 minute sessions worrying about the tumor. I'll discuss this important aspect in a later chapter).

Now, Hold Off A Minute Kiddo

If you've read other Mind Power/Self Improvement/Law of Attraction experts I know what you're dying to tell me…

"Hey Todd, you're not supposed to mention diseases by name when you're trying to heal them because you're focusing on a disease...something negative."

This is one of the things that makes my message different from those claims. I'll address that later. But for now, let's continue...OK?

However, here's the good news. Developing Your Power is a skill that doesn't take as long to master as learning how to play a musical instrument well, or becoming a great artist or athlete, or other skills that take years to develop.

I can't give you a time frame as to how long it will take you to master it because it depends on how much time and effort you spend practicing, and how strong your belief in it is.

But if you make a genuine effort and practice it as I'm showing you and don't give up after several tries and accept the fact that it does work, you'll be amazed at how quickly you'll start to see results. In a later chapter I'll show you how you can "jump start" the process so Your Power will work very easily. It will give you "Super Mind Power".

Too Much Of A Good Thing?

But what exactly do I mean by repetition? And how much is enough? Can you do it too much?

Dr. Joseph Murphy in his classic book, *"The Power of Your Subconscious Mind"* says too much effort can stifle results. I tend to agree when using your Mind Power to attract things, such as wealth, success, a soul mate.

So to be successful in your career or to attract anything else you want – money or a soul mate, for instance -- try doing a 15 to 20 minute affirmation session. Say your affirmation over and over again during that time (there's some repetition) and then don't think about it the rest of the day.

But don't begin to worry about the reasons you started to do the affirmation…not being successful, not having money, not having a soul mate. If you do start to worry later in the day, start to say some lines from the affirmation for a few minutes to keep those negative thoughts out of your mind.

And just as defeating would be asking yourself…

"*well, when's it going to work?*"

That's reinforcing in your Subconscious Mind that you don't yet have what you're affirming, and you'll start to doubt the power you have.

I've done a 15 minute affirmation session just once a day for several mornings, and without thinking about it the rest of the day I saw results within a few days.

So consistency is the key…15-20 minutes (over and over again) and every day until you reach your goal (there's some more repetition). If using your Mind Power to attain a goal, you'll get there faster if you use Your Power every day until you reach it. Stating your affirmation one day, then skipping several days, then saying it for a few days then skipping a few will only slow you down.

Keep this in mind if you want to learn a skill such as playing golf, playing a musical instrument or becoming an artist. Practice the skill, *PLUS* incorporate using Your Power every day by imagining you're great at it now. Imagine you're executing every mechanic as well as you need to in order to be great. You'll master the skill quicker than if you just practice manually.

In that university study I mentioned a few pages ago…about one group of students shooting basketballs while another group only imagined they were shooting baskets. I wish they had included a fourth group… students who had practiced manually *AND* spent time imagining they were practicing and sinking every shot. Undoubtedly, that group would have improved the most.

Key #4 - The Subconscious Mind only thinks in infinite or absolute terms

It doesn't think in finite or partial terms as the conscious mind can. So when using Your Power avoid numbers. They're finite terms.

Don't affirm…

"I'm a millionaire"…

but affirm something such as…

"I have all the money I need…way more than I'll ever need for myself."

I'll explain this **Key** further as we go through the book.

Key #5 - Your Subconscious Mind works quicker at getting you what you want if when saying affirmations you feel the emotion you would feel if you had it.

And this **Key** hammers home my two-sentence message near the beginning of this chapter about tricking the Subconscious Mind into believing you have NOW what you want.

Let's use the brain tumor example again. If your doctor says…

"The tumor in your brain is gone and you're now cancer free"…

how would you feel? Happy, ecstatic, relieved, like a huge weight has been lifted from you, like you got a new lease on life?

Of course you would. All of that and then some. You might want to go out and celebrate by painting the town or throwing yourself a big party with friends and family.

So when using your Subconscious Mind to dissolve the tumor from your brain, say…

"The tumor in my brain has dissolved away and I'm free of cancer"…

but also say it with feeling. Feel all those wonderful and happy emotions you would feel when being told by your doctor you're cancer free.

Just imagine those feelings, feel those feelings, put a big smile on your face, laugh out loud or cry tears of joy, pretend you're an actor portraying a character who has learned s/he is cancer free.

Or whatever goal you're trying to attain, feel the emotion of finally having it while saying your affirmation.

Feeling the emotions you would feel if you had what you're affirming will trick the Subconscious Mind into believing you have it NOW. Then your Subconscious Mind will see it and deliver it to you.

Key #6 - Your conscious mind is your logical, rational, analytical, judgmental mind.

It will never accept an idea that doesn't make 100% logical/rational sense. If you were about to accept an idea but noticed one little part didn't make logical sense – let's say just 1% of the idea sounds "screwy" -- you would stop and think or say something such as...

"*wait a minute, that doesn't add up.*"

You would question it, think about it for a while, analyze it, try to make sense out of it and try to come to some kind of logical conclusion about it.

And if you couldn't you most likely would reject the entire idea, at least until you could rationalize some kind of sense out of that one little part that "doesn't add up."

But your Subconscious Mind is your il-logical, ir-rational, non-analytical, non-judgmental mind.

And this is what you need to know for you to take Your Power to incredible heights, beyond achieving merely average results but going into greatness. You do that by setting your sights beyond your conscious, or logical limitations.

That's because the Subconscious will believe ***ANYTHING*** whether it makes logical/rational sense or not. It never analyzes or questions anything you tell it as your conscious mind does.

This is probably the biggest stumbling block that keeps people from trying to learn how to harness their Mind Power to acquire things such as wealth or possessions, or to rid the body of disease or to prevent disease. They can't see the logic to it. In their conscious mind, "it doesn't add up."

Does it make logical sense that imagining a tumor in your brain is gone will make it go away? Of course not.

But your Subconscious Mind is not logical…it's il-logical. You can't make logical sense out of something that's il-logical.

That's why the medical community is skeptical about using one's Mind Power to cure diseases. Doctors are scientists. Before a treatment is accepted as effective it has to undergo rigorous testing for years and be logically and scientifically proved.

But you can prove to yourself the effectiveness of Your Power in a much shorter time period than science needs to prove its theories.

Let me prove my point that the Subconscious Mind is il-logical by sharing an experience I had. I used to be a telemarketer, and I can hear you right now…

"Oh no, he was one of those annoying guys who always calls me during dinner?"

Yeah, yeah. Sorry. I needed a gig, you dig?

We used the term "Laydown". That's a person who accepts an offer without ever saying "Not interested". They listen to the presentation and the first thing they say is…

"O-kay, I'll take it"…

thereby not requiring the telemarketer to use rebuttals to try to turn a "Not Interested" into a "Yes". The customer "lays down for you."

Nowadays, most telemarketers sit at a computer wearing a headset while the computer quickly dials the phone numbers of all the customers in the data base. When a customer picks up their phone and says "Hello", voice contact is made, the computer stops dialing, the marketer hears a BEEP in their headset signaling them to start talking, and the customer's information such as name and address appears on the monitor.

On this particular day, it was the first day of the month when we'd get a new list of prospects. After 90 minutes I had talked to 26 prospects. All of them said "Not interested", and I couldn't turn any of them around.

So I punched off the clock, went to my car and for about 15 minutes I said over and over again…

"*I'm the best sales rep that* (Company name) *ever had. Every customer who comes to my phone is a lay down. My computer knows who all the lay downs are and sends them to my phone. Customers never tell me they're not interested. I never have to give rebuttals because the people who my computer sends me are predisposed to get it anyway, no matter which sales rep they talk to. I'm just lucky enough that my computer knows who the lay downs are and sends them to me.*"

I punched back in the clock, went back to work and in the first hour I got 4 sales all lay downs. The next hour I got 3 sales, all lay downs. The shift was 6 hours. To earn bonus money I needed to finish with 6 sales, one sale an hour. I had one more than I needed after two hours.

Now, was it rational for me to think that a computer knows which customers out of thousands of names in a data base are predisposed to accept an offer without ever once saying "not interested" and can send them to my phone? Was it rational for me to think that by saying what

I did, my computer – a machine – would respond according to how I imagined it could?

Of course not. But as I've said, your Subconscious Mind is not rational or logical. It's ir-rational or il-logical.

Was it also rational for me to think that EVERY customer I spoke to would be a lay down? No. I talked to 10 customers the first hour and got 4 sales. 4 out of ten is a good conversion rate, especially when I only needed to average one sale an hour to make bonus money, and that I didn't get any sales out of 26 attempts before I did the affirmation.

This is an example of **Key #4** – The Subconscious Mind only thinks in infinite or absolute terms, not in finite or partial terms.

I didn't affirm...

"*I get 4 sales every hour.*"

Numbers are finite or partial terms or ideas in which the Subconscious Mind doesn't think. "EVERY" is an infinite or absolute term.

I shared this skill with a fellow telemarketer named Brian. He had been struggling to get sales. After just a few days of doing the affirmation I did in my car for 15 minutes, his sales started to take off. And most of them were lay downs. He said before he started to use his Mind Power, he had to fight to get the few sales he got and use rebuttals to turn the "not interested's" into sales (like those typical telemarketers).

Can you make logical sense out of the experience I just shared with you? Can you logically explain why after 90 minutes I couldn't get one lay down or even one sale using a rebuttal after speaking to 26 customers... then for 15 minutes I imagine my computer knows who the lay downs are and sends 7 of them to my phone in 2 hours. And without changing my sales approach at all?

Or why in just a few days Brian started to get more sales – mostly "lay downs" – after struggling to get the few he got? And without changing his sales approach?

You can't, can you? And no scientist will be able to logically or rationally explain it either. But I don't have to spend time trying to figure it out or rationalizing it and it doesn't boggle my mind anymore because I know it works.

And that's what you have to do…know that it works. Accept it. Take it for granted that it works. Prove to yourself that it works.

By understanding that your Subconscious Mind is not logical or rational…that it will believe <u>ANYTHING</u> whether it makes logical, rational sense or not…that it <u>NEVER</u> questions, analyzes or rationalizes anything you tell it will help convince you of its power. That's one thing that makes it powerful…it's not confined to the boundaries of logic as the conscious mind is.

Now you know how the Subconscious Mind works. You now know more about it than most people ever will…even more than some gurus. Consider yourself an expert.

Still to come, I will share with you another element to what I believe makes my message different than that of many Self Improvement authorities.

You're going to learn how to go beyond achieving realistic goals by developing your ***<u>Extreme Mind Power</u>***.

CHAPTER 4

"Speak Softly...But Carry A Big Can Of Paint"

~Banksy, anonymous England-based street artist, vandal, political activist, and film director

I like that quote by Banksy and feel it's appropriate because what we believe and say about ourselves "paint" our minds with either positive or negative thoughts. And saying affirmations is how you're going to "paint" your mind as you begin to harness Your Power.

You can buy books of pre-written affirmations. But I want to teach you how to write your own. No one knows what you want and need more than you. Plus, now that you've learned how the Subconscious Mind works you can write powerful affirmations tailor made to help you get just about anything you want.

I've read books that claim affirmations are more effective when said out loud. I see their point, but I've never said them out loud. Just saying them in my head has worked well for me. Feel free to say them out loud if that works better for you.

To show you how to write your affirmations correctly, I'll write one that you can use as a model to follow. Let's say you want to use Your Power to be better at your career. I can't give you an affirmation for every career because I haven't had every career imaginable. So I'll give you one example you can use to help formulate an affirmation for the type of work you do. All you have to do is change the words to fit your situation.

First, sit down with a pen and piece of paper. Write down the important elements of your job. List all the things you need to do well in order to do well in your job.

Be specific and very detailed. The Subconscious Mind works better that way. So stay away from generalities. That goes for any affirmation for any situation.

So you have your list. Doesn't it make sense that if you do all of those elements better you'll be better at your career? Of course. So you want to make sure you include all of those elements in your affirmation.

I know something about "Outside Sales". That's a job in which a salesperson calls businesses, sets up appointments with them and then goes "outside of their office" to meet with them and tries to turn those prospects into clients. Most companies call those salespeople Account Executives.

One example would be a computer salesman who calls on businesses trying to sell them his/her company's line of computers, then continues to service those accounts when clients have questions, problems, or want to upgrade the system.

Salespeople say these are some keys to being a good salesperson:

1. Make the prospect feel you're helping them get what *they* want. If they feel you're trying to get what *you* want, the prospect will be less likely to buy from you.

2. If you're in sales because you like helping and serving people by selling them products or services that will make their job easier

and help their company be more productive and profitable...if you enjoy hearing from your clients how much your product or service has helped them by increasing their company's business and that's what drives your ambition, then the money you can make will happen. If you're driven mainly by the money you can make, money will probably be harder to come by.

3. When meeting with prospects trying to win them as clients, act the same as they do. "Mirror" their body language, tempo of their speech, tone of their voice, mannerisms. This subconsciously conveys to the prospect..."I'm just like you. You can trust me."

If I were a computer salesman, this is how I would write my affirmation.

"I am the greatest computer salesman who ever lived. Every call I make to a prospect ends up with a sale on my first visit. The prospect always accepts my offer before listening to presentations by computer salesmen from other companies. Every prospect is eager to buy our computers on my first visit. I'm able to convince the prospect so easily that they're getting a great deal and they feel very good about our computers because they can tell right away that our computers and the service I can provide them are going to help them in their job, and will make their company more profitable. Every prospect likes and trusts me and can see right away that our computers can help them serve their clients so much faster and better and their business will increase. When I meet with a prospect, I always mirror their actions and they get a real good feeling about me because they can tell I'm just like them and they trust me. They can really tell I'm trying to help them get what they want. I love doing sales because I'm making my clients' job easier and helping their company become more productive and profitable. It's such a great feeling to hear from my clients about how their business has really picked up since they became my client. And when they call me with a question or a need, it's such a great feeling to be able to be of service to them."

I could make this even more powerful by imagining I'm seeing all this happen. I would pause during my affirmation and imagine I'm in the prospect's office and he/she is smiling and eagerly listening while I do my presentation, and he/she says...

"Hey, I think these computers are exactly what we've been looking for. These will work out great. I want to get them right away."

Or when I affirm...

"I love hearing from my clients about how our computers have helped them..."

I would pause and imagine the client calls me to say...

"Hey Todd, those computers are great. And that program you gave us has already helped us pick up 5 new clients and our business is really taking off now"...

and I would imagine feeling happy for them.

So visualization is another key component in harnessing Your Power. See what it is that you're affirming. Get it set in your mind.

Notice that the three "keys to selling" listed above are included in the affirmation. Now, let's examine the affirmation to see that it addresses **The 6 Keys:**

Key #1 - The Subconscious Mind only thinks in the present

I am stating everything in the present, aren't I? Look at the first sentence of the affirmation...

"I AM the greatest computer salesman who ever lived"...

not...

"I'm GOING to be the greatest computer salesman someday."

Or...

"I'm GOING to get a lot of sales today."

Key #2 - The Subconscious Mind does not know the difference between what is real and what is imagined

I am imagining all this and I'm tricking my Subconscious Mind into believing it even more by visualizing the entire scenario. I'm seeing the prospect acting favorably during my presentation, and hearing him/her say...

"I'm going to get these computers now."

Plus, I'm tricking my Subconscious Mind into believing it's happening still more by incorporating **Key #5 – Feel The Emotion**. As I'm doing my affirmation, I'm feeling all the emotions I would feel if all those things I affirmed were really happening.

Key #3 - The Subconscious Mind learns by repetition

If you're just starting to develop your new skill of harnessing your power, you couldn't say an affirmation such as the example I used just once for one or two minutes and have it work.

And remember my telemarketing colleague Brian I told you about in the previous chapter? He just did the affirmation in the morning for 15 to 20 minutes without thinking about it the rest of the day. Within just several days his sales started to increase. And that was his first attempt at using his Mind Power.

So repetition...over and over again until the goal is attained.

Key #6 - The Subconscious Mind is ir-rational/il-logical

Look at the second sentence of the affirmation:

"EVERY call I make to a prospect ends up with a sale on my first visit."

Is it rational to think I would get a sale on my first visit to a prospect EVERY time? Of course not.

But my Subconscious Mind is not going to think...

"Whoa, you want to make a sale on your first trip EVERY TIME? Wow, that's really asking a lot. I doubt I can do that for you...maybe every other time or most of the time, but EVERY time?"

Remember that your Subconscious Mind never questions what you tell it, so don't set your sights low. Set them high. The sky's the limit, think as big as you can, shoot for the stars, "go for the gusto."

If I affirm that I get a sale on my first visit with EVERY prospect (**Key #4** – the Subconscious Mind only thinks in infinite or absolute terms, not in finite or partial terms), I'll get a lot more sales than if I affirm "MOST" prospects. Maybe I'll get a sale on the first or second visit 40, 50, or 65% of the time (or at least more than I would if I didn't use My Power). For any salesperson, that would be an awesome conversion rate. If I affirm I get a sale on the first visit MOST of the time I'll greatly diminish my results. Here's why:

First of all, "MOST" is a partial term, in which the Subconscious Mind doesn't think. Plus, I've read books in which the author says your Subconscious Mind Power works only to the extent that you believe in it.

I disagree. If you believe in it halfway (partially) it won't work for you just 50 percent of the time. It won't work at all because the other 50% of the time you'll doubt that it works. Doubt will negate your half-hearted effort.

Key #4 - Your Subconscious Mind only thinks in absolutes, not in partials.

When you affirm something, affirm it as ALWAYS being true, not MOST OF THE TIME as true. You have to believe in Your Power 100% of the time for you to master it. Think in terms of those Frank Sinatra classics…"All The Way" and "All Or Nothing At All".

A Few More Important Tidbits

Don't be concerned if you repeat things while you're affirming. Just keep saying your affirmation over and over again for a good 15 – 20 minutes. Then don't think about it again the rest of the day. Don't overdo it. I want you to see how easy it really is to harness your Mind Power.

But more importantly…don't start to think negatively about your goal during the day, such as worrying about not reaching it or thinking any other negative thoughts that will keep the new program from taking hold.

If you do start to worry, then start to say lines from your affirmation for a few minutes to block out the negativity. Don't undo what you're trying to accomplish.

Putting Pen To Paper

So now that you know how the Subconscious Mind thinks and you know how to formulate a properly stated affirmation, it's time for you to write one of your own.

I want you to think of a goal you want to attain and I want it to be a big goal, the biggest one you can think of…the thing that's most important to you, the thing you want more than any other thing you can think of... but one that you can see you're getting close to reaching within a few weeks, even if it's just one or two steps.

And be specific, not...

"I just want to be happy and live a long and happy life."

Getting better at your current career is an excellent goal to use for this assignment as opposed to something such as...

"I want to win Judy's/Bob's heart and marry him/her."

If Judy/Bob doesn't love you or even worse hates your guts, that would be a hard goal to accomplish.

That's something that's possible for more advanced Mind Power practitioners and later on we'll be discussing how to use Your Power to attract a soul mate, even if s/he currently doesn't love you. But for this assignment choose a goal you can obtain without needing the heart's desire of someone else.

So choose a goal that's very important to you…one for which you have a lot of passion. And make it something you're involved in on a regular basis such as your job or a hobby...something in which you can see that you're getting better at within a few weeks after you start to program your Subconscious Mind.

Doing extremely well in a career is not a good choice for this purpose if it's a career you can't have for a long time such as…becoming a great medical doctor but you're a first year college student. That's a goal you can't attain now because of the many years of schooling you have to go through first.

A better example of a career goal would be if you're, let's say…a commissioned sales person. In such a career you can start to see your sales increase within the next few weeks or so and continue to improve.

Or perhaps you're a writer and in a few weeks you can feel your writing is flowing more easily, words are coming to you quicker, your writing is quick and snappy.

If your career doesn't provide such a goal then choose a hobby you're very passionate about. Let's say you play golf and want to be great at it...even if you don't plan to become a professional. Or you love to play the piano and you want to play it very well...again, even if you have no plans to make it your profession.

Make the example of my affirmation fit your goal. Just change the words to fit yours. And throughout your Mind Power session sprinkle in some visualizations. Imagine you're doing what you're affirming. If you want to be great at golf, imagine you're playing it and hitting the ball longer than you've ever hit it...and sinking the longest putts you've ever made.

If you want to be a great musician imagine you're great at it NOW and can see that you're getting better at it within a few weeks.

If you want to be a writer or artist imagine you are NOW and great ideas are flowing to you effortlessly.

And as you see yourself improving in the goal you chose continue with the daily 15 to 20 minutes Mind Power session for a good two months. This is extremely important as you'll learn later on.

OK? See what I mean? Ya dig me, man? Are you hip to what I'm saying?

Great! Oh, I'm really having a lot of fun, aren't you? I'm really enjoying the time we're spending together. I love sharing this "stuff" with people. And I'm really looking forward to hearing from you how your life has improved because of what I've shown you.

And what I'm going to show you next is how to use "A Big Can Of Paint" as Banksy says because you're going to start your Mind Power development by thinking BIG!

CHAPTER 5

Aim High - Beyond Realistic Goals

Just as a reminder...whatever goal you choose to begin your Mind Power development it must be one you have a great deal of passion for…one that's very important to you…one that you want to greatly attain and offers you the chance to see that you're making strides in reaching within the next several weeks, your job or a hobby that you love.

We're not going to start off by me telling you to…

"set small, realistic goals and try to accomplish them one step at a time and the bigger, long term goals will eventually take care of themselves"...

as many other self improvement experts teach. You can go about it that way if you want but it will take you longer to reach your goals and develop your Mind Power ability. And it will just get you average results. But you want to be great don't you?

So you're going to start off ***BIG*** by "going for the gusto" from the beginning, by "shooting for the stars" right out of the gate, by "setting your sites" as high as you can NOW...using that "Big Can Of Paint" as Banksy says.

In other words, set and go after ***ambitious*** goals. Only that way can you go beyond mediocrity into greatness.

Setting ambitious goals requires a lot of ambition to achieve them which in turn sparks your ambition, thereby taking you to greater heights than do realistic ones.

Proof I'm Correct

I always knew I was right about this concept, especially now that there's scientific evidence to back up my claim.

Studies published online in the *Journal of Consumer Research* say those who set and attain ambitious goals are more satisfied in life than those who set less ambitious ones...goals they know ahead of time they will be likely to achieve...in other words, "realistic, easily attainable" goals.

Professor Cecile K. Cho of the University of California-Riverside -- who conducted two of the studies -- says...

"The moral of the story is don't sell yourself short. Aim high."[2]

Results of the study - according to social psychologist Heidi G. Halvorson, Ph.D. – are consistent with research on personal and professional goal-setting.

Author of the book...*"Succeed: How We Can Reach Our Goals"*, Dr. Halvorson says we set goals with two factors in mind: (1) *expectancy* – how likely we believe we'll succeed at achieving them. And (2) *value* -- how good it will be for us if we reach them.

"Safe bets, generally speaking, are less valuable ones," she says. *"So once you've achieved the relatively easy goal, it's only natural to think about what it has cost you in terms of value -- and that's going to reduce your satisfaction."*[3]

Extreme Mind Power

I agree totally with what those two ladies say. But I want you to take your Mind Power to the extreme...beyond what they say. Go beyond attaining ambitious goals by tricking your Subconscious into believing you've attained ***extreme*** goals...even ***impossible*** goals.

I said in **Key #6** that the Subconscious Mind is not confined to the boundaries of logic as the conscious mind is. And that it will believe ANYTHING you tell it whether it makes logical sense or not.

So don't confine your affirmations to the boundaries of logic. Make your affirmations...*IL-LOGICAL.* Trick your Subconscious into believing that you've attained "unrealistic goals"...ones that in the real world would be impossible to reach.

Let's say you want to be a great baseball player. Program your Subconscious Mind by affirming everyday for 15-20 minutes something such as...

"I'm the greatest baseball player who ever lived. With every swing of the bat I hit the ball out of the ballpark."

In the real world, that's an unrealistic, impossible goal. No one – not even Barry Bonds, nor Hall of Famers Babe Ruth, Hank Aaron or Willie Mays – hit homers with every swing of the bat. The greatest home run hitters of the day can't do that in the Home Run Derby the night before the All Star game when they're *trying* to hit a homer on every swing... when they're getting a much slower pitch than they get in a real game. They even know what type of pitch is coming because the guy pitching to them is the one they practiced with to prepare for the Derby.

Will you hit a homer with every swing of the bat if you program your Subconscious with such an affirmation? In your Subconscious you will. In the real world, however...ABSOLUTELY NOT!!!

So why program your Subconscious with a goal that's impossible to attain in the real world? By doing so -- aiming high, thinking big, unrealistically, illogically, ***extremely***, using *"A Big Can Of Paint"* and using absolute terms (with *every* swing) -- you'll go beyond being a mediocre player...even beyond being a good player...to becoming a GREAT...even an EXTREMELY great player.

You will hit many more homers than you would if you only practiced hitting without using your Mind Power...or practiced manually and also programmed your Subconscious Mind with a more "realistic" goal such as...hitting a homer every 8 games (and using a finite term – 8 --in which the Subconscious doesn't think...not a good choice of terms).

If you want to be a great musician and the first day of learning your new craft you affirm...

"I'm the greatest musician who ever lived"...

your Subconscious Mind is not going to think...

"Hey wait a minute. You want me to make you the greatest musician NOW? Gee, I don't know if I can do that. It's too early for that. You just started to learn (whatever instrument). *It's going to take some time for me to get you there. Let's take it one day at a time and see where you are in 6 months."*

Your *conscious* mind will think that. But you're trying to program your Subconscious Mind, not your conscious mind.

Let's say your goal is to work for yourself as a personal fitness trainer. It's good to write down goals such as...

"I want to have 2 clients by my first month, then 3 clients by the second month, then 5 clients by the third month," etc., etc...

because we know in the real world – in our conscious mind -- that's how it happens.

Writing down your goals stating what you want to accomplish and by when gives you a road map to follow...a destination to get you to. It keeps you on track in striving for a goal.

But when you program your Subconscious Mind to grow your business and accomplish your goals, don't affirm...

"*My business is going great. I get 2 new clients every month.*"

First of all, "2 clients" and "months" are finite terms in which the Subconscious Mind doesn't think. Write your "realistic goals" on paper.

But to achieve them faster and greater than you had planned, affirm in your Subconscious Mind from the first day of marketing your service...

"*My business is going great. I have many, many clients...way more than I thought I would ever get. People are signing up for my service in droves. I attract clients to me all the time. And all my clients refer their friends and relatives to me. It's such a great feeling to be helping so many people reach their fitness goals.*"

And feel the emotions you would feel if that really had happened.

Let's say you wrote down a goal to have 10 clients by the sixth month. If you affirm it in your Subconscious Mind the way I suggested, you might have that many by the fourth or third month...maybe even the second month.

Is it rational to think that you can do an affirmation once for 15 minutes and then have what you want right away? No! But your Subconscious Mind is not rational.

Don't get caught up trying to rationalize something that's irrational. Or trying to make logical sense out of something that's illogical. The sooner your Subconscious believes what you tell it, the sooner it will deliver it to you.

If your goal is your dream job, see yourself in it when saying the affirmation. If that job would require you to wear a suit every day, dress that way now if you can. If possible, dress whatever way your dream job would require you to dress. Start to convince your Subconscious Mind you have that job NOW!

So set big goals knowing that it takes time to reach them. Program your Subconscious Mind for "extreme" results. Do that while knowing you're only trying to reach your goal faster and greater...trying to go from mediocrity into greatness. Don't get discouraged if you don't reach your goal on the first try, or don't hit a homer with every swing when you're actually playing a game.

Phew! Glad That's Off My Chest

I wanted to blow the lid off commonly held beliefs about setting goals and how to use your Mind Power to achieve them and show you what I think is one of the teachings that makes my message different from that of the established Gurus who teach…"one step at a time", and…"set realistic goals." It's one of my "Soap Boxes."

But there's still something ***more*** you can do to get even greater results from your efforts than what I've taught you in this chapter. That's... *"Still To Come"* as they say on TV newscasts.

So get your affirmation on paper. Use the one I wrote as a guide to write your own. Make sure it follows **The 6 Keys.**

Avoid saying finite or partial terms (numbers or words like "most", or "sometimes"). Talk in absolute or infinite terms **(Key #4)**.

Spend a good 15-20 minutes saying the affirmation...over and over again. Allow those thoughts to "simmer" or "marinate" in your Subconscious. This is how you go beyond Positive Thinking.

When you're finished, don't think about it the rest of the day. I want you to see how easy it is to harness Your Power...provided you say the affirmation every day. If you don't see results after a week or two, try a second affirmation session later in the day.

And just as important, *DO NOT* start to worry about the reason you're saying the affirmation, for example...worrying about reaching it. If that happens, STOP and say some lines from the affirmation for a few minutes to get those negative thoughts out of your mind.

So go ahead and pick your goal and write your affirmation. But don't start to program your Subconscious Mind just yet. Wait until after you read the next chapter.

CHAPTER 6

The Gateway To Your Mind Power

This is how you get extreme results in improving your life and attaining your desires, by programming the Subconscious Mind whereas many standard methods such as Positive Thinking and setting and achieving goals are conducted on the conscious level.

And here's a tip for programming your Subconscious to bring about your desires:

"It is in the Silence that you get in touch with the Omnipotent power of the subconscious mind from which all power is evolved."
~ Charles Haanel, New Thought author.

The above quote reflects the first part of Banksy's quote for the title of Chapter 4:

"Speak Softly..."

I've said previously that developing Your Power takes time, practice and effort. But not strenuous effort. DO NOT use force to bring about the desires you're seeking. Speaking softly to your Subconscious Mind is all it takes. But keep the other Keys in play, especially #5 - *"Feel The Emotion You'd Feel If You Already Had What You're Affirming."*

Before you begin a session of programming your Subconscious Mind you want to relax your body because you also want to relax your mind.

Clear all the junk out of the way and get your brain wave activity to a minimum so you can focus on the ONE thing on which you want to focus. The Subconscious Mind is more susceptible to receiving and acting upon suggestions when it's relaxed and focused on that one thing. And it's easier for it to focus when it's relaxed.

Any kind of relaxation works for this. If you're into Transcendental Meditation, that will work fine. When you get to the point that you would start to say your Mantra, say the affirmation.

Or just imagine that relaxation is spreading from the top of your head down to and out from the tips of your fingers and toes...and feel your muscles are relaxing. Just imagine it.

Here's how I do my relaxation. First, I put on some very relaxing music… not too loud, just in the background. This is optional. Try using music at first to see if it helps you relax. If you relax easier without it, don't use music. But you want your surroundings to be quiet (except for the music if you use it). If you have a family, tell your spouse and children or whoever else is in your dwelling not to bother you for the next 20 minutes or for however long you plan to spend. And before you begin, tell whoever is there to take a message if you get a phone call.

I sit in a reclining chair and breathe at a normal pace for about 30 seconds and get my mind off of things. Then I take a deep breath, hold it for 5 seconds, then slowly exhale and as I do, I imagine my body is becoming relaxed, as if it's drifting down to the next level. Then I return to normal breathing for about 10 seconds, imagining that my breathing is slightly lighter than it was when I started. I repeat that process 4 or 5 times, then while I exhale the last time I close my eyes and say to myself softly and slowly…

"The muscles around my eyes are totally and completely relaxed...I couldn't open my eyes if I wanted to because the muscles are soooo relaxed...now I see coming from the sky a beam of light, shining on the muscles around my eyes relaxing them even further...the light of relaxation is penetrating deeply into every muscle, nerve and fiber around my eyes, making them even more relaxed...my breathing is soooo light, my heart and pulse are beating sooooo slowly...now the light of relaxation is spreading from my eyes down my face, down to my jaw and all the surrounding area...down my neck and around to the back of my neck...now the light of relaxation is spreading down my back, down past my shoulder blades...now the light of relaxation has spread across my back, out to the sides of my torso...now the light of relaxation continues down my back and sides, penetrating deeply into the nerves, muscles and fibers, relaxing them even more...all the way down to the small of my back...down to my waist...now the light of relaxation is shining on the sides of my neck and has spread across the top of my shoulders, just relaxing them...now the light of relaxation is moving slowly down my arms, penetrating deeply into every nerve, muscle and fiber making them soooo relaxed...and now the light has gone down to my elbows and has relaxed every muscle...now the light of relaxation is moving down my forearms...slowly down...into my wrists...hands... fingers...and all the way out through the tips of my fingers...now the light of relaxation is shining on the front of my neck and is moving down my chest area, penetrating deeply into every muscle, nerve and fiber...past my chest area...and all the way down to my solar plexus...now down to my abdomen and all the surrounding area...down to my waist...now the light of relaxation shines on my pelvis and hips and is moving down to my thighs...it continues down my thighs relaxing every muscle, nerve and fiber...alllllll the way down to my knees...now the relaxation continues down my calves...cascading down to my ankles...into my feet...and all the way out through the tips of my toes...every part of my body is totally, and completely relaxed."

At this point you're ready to begin programming your Subconscious Mind. Say your affirmation over and over for 15-20 minutes. Don't be concerned that you repeat things. Remember **Key #3**, Repetition.

When you're finished with the Mind Power session, don't jump up and out of your seat and be raring to go. Since your breathing, heartbeat, metabolism and circulation have slowed way down during this time -- plus your mind and body being in a very deep state of relaxation for 15 to 20 minutes – you want to gradually bring those systems back to the point where they were before you started the relaxation. If you don't you could get a bit dizzy or feel light-headed when you get out of your seat.

Spend about 30 seconds getting your system back to normal. Start to wiggle your toes for about 5 seconds, then your fingers. Feel your circulation gradually picking back up. Make your breathing gradually more pronounced. You won't be in a different state of mind when you're harnessing Your Power. You'll just be in a very deep state of relaxation, so you want your body and mind to feel as if they're coming back to the surface.

Now, as I said, that's how I do it. If this works for you, great. If not, you can do it the way that works best for you. But you want to get your body totally relaxed. You don't have to make an effort to relax your mind. It will relax along with your body.

And don't rush through this. I spend about 5 minutes doing the relaxation. Spend at least that amount of time.

Also, I recommend that you do this in the morning before you go to work. If you do it in the evening after working all day and then eating dinner, you may fall asleep and miss out on practicing your new skill and throw your night sleep schedule off. So try it at a time when you're less likely to fall asleep. And do it in a sitting position.

I also recommend doing it on an empty stomach or waiting at least an hour after eating a big meal. If you do it right after eating, the food will sit in your stomach like a blob because your metabolism will drastically slow down.

And notice where I put three dots...That's where you pause and imagine that part of your body relaxing. Just imagine it, pretend your body is relaxing...feel your muscles relaxing. Then move on to the next area to be relaxed.

Don't try to memorize this. Record your voice saying the relaxation. Play it back and follow along that way. Use a small tape recorder or any device that has a "Pause" button you can push during those spots when you want to pause and feel your muscles relaxing. Place the device on your lap. Then release the "Pause" button when you're ready to move the relaxation to the next body part. After doing the relaxation a number of times, you'll have it memorized.

The Conscious Mind Is *MORE* Involved

You'll hear many gurus claim that by doing the relaxation that I described above you're getting the conscious mind "out of the way" so your thoughts bypass the conscious mind and go straight to the Subconscious.

Any hypnotherapist will tell you that when you are "hypnotized", you're merely in a very deep state of relaxation. And during that time you're awake and very aware of your surroundings. That's because your conscious mind is more heightened and very "in tune" with what's going on during that time (I discuss self-hypnosis next chapter).

With relaxation you're involving the conscious mind MORE so it can greatly process your affirmation. And that way your Subconscious can then really "drink in" your message and act upon it.

I'm sorry if I'm making the relaxation process seem more difficult than it is and that you think it's very difficult to master. It's not. It's a very natural process. I just wanted to clear up a few misconceptions about it.

So don't put a lot of strenuous effort into this. Just feel your muscles relaxing gently, effortlessly… naturally... *"allllll the way down."*

How Low Must You Go?

You'll find websites that offer software that claims to make you so relaxed that you get your brain waves extremely low, down to the beta level, alpha level and so on so you can harness your Mind Power.

While I don't doubt their software can do the things they claim -- nor do I doubt their claims of the benefits one can receive by getting the mind to those levels -- it's really not necessary for when you want to program your Subconscious Mind.

Before I learned how to use My Power I used to think that in order to tap into it you'd have to get…"way down to the very depths of your psyche."

But you don't. Your Mind Power is right beneath the surface…just one step down from your conscious level. Relaxation helps you get to it. It is…"The Gateway To Your Mind Power."

STOP!!!

Before you read any further, I need to explain something. In Part One I showed you how to harness Your Power by programming your Subconscious Mind.

The following parts show you many different ways in which you can use Your Power. If you haven't reached the goal you chose, go ahead and read Parts Two and Three but DO NOT try any of the examples I show you just yet. They can be used any time in the future and don't have anything to do with achieving your goal. I don't want multiple Mind Power messages jamming your Subconscious and getting in the way of achieving the goal. This is very important as you will see later on.

PART 2

Your Mind Power For Everything

CHAPTER 7

EVERYTHING? Well, Just About

Have you reached your goal? Great. I'm so happy for you. You have taken a big step, a huge leap in learning about yourself and the power and natural abilities you have. I'm so glad you trusted me with bringing that out of you.

If you haven't reached it yet, keep at it. If you chose the right goal – something you can see yourself starting to attain within a few weeks – you should be reaching it shortly. Making just the slightest advancement toward reaching it will convince you of the power you inherently possess.

Listen Up, Please

Before I resume showing you how powerful your Mind Power is I need to clarify something. You've noticed how I say you can use your Your Power to get just about anything you want. Your Power is not absolute because you can only use it to acquire what's possible within The Laws of the Universe.

For example…if heaven forbid you're in a serious accident or you have diabetes and must have a leg amputated, you can't use your Mind Power to grow another one. It's not within our makeup to re-grow limbs. That could be changing in the future with developing research into stem cell re-growth, but that's for later.

However, while you're somewhat limited as to what you can acquire with Your Power, you're going to learn there are many, many situations you can use it to get just about anything you want. Here are just a few examples.

An Introduction To The LOA

Well, guess what? Practice harnessing your Mind Power to get what you want and you will take the first step to mastering The Law of Attraction. You won't have to purchase and study another book for that. You've been learning about The Law of Attraction the entire time. But to get it to work on autopilot there's another important element you must incorporate. I'll talk about that part of it in an upcoming chapter.

What your mind focuses on is what you attract. That can result in something either good or bad. If you do affirmations correctly to get something you want, that's what you'll get. If you focus on something you do not want to have happen – known as *"WORRYING"* – that's what you'll get. In either case the Subconscious Mind worked the same way…the one and only way it knows how to work.

When you use affirmations correctly to get what you want, you have tricked the Subconscious Mind into believing you have it NOW. When you worry about something, you're thinking in the present **(Key #1)**. You're imagining your worry has come to be. You've tricked the Subconscious Mind into believing it has happened NOW because when you worry, you're also feeling the emotions you would feel if that worry were a reality **(Key #5 – feel the emotion).**

That's why I've stressed that if you say an affirmation to get something and later in the day you start to worry about the reasons that prompted you to say it -- lack of money, for example – it's important to stop worrying and start to say lines from the affirmation for a few minutes to keep those negative thoughts at bay.

Attracting Wealth

Let's say you want to be wealthy. Wealth is a state of mind, just as poverty is. So that means you can use your Mind Power to acquire wealth. Just formulate an affirmation.

"I'm surrounded by wealth. Money flows to me constantly. I have way more than I'll ever need for myself. I give of my money freely, and what I give away comes back to me multiplied many times over. Money follows me wherever I go. I attract money to me like a magnet."

You can formulate your own affirmation. Just use your imagination. Avoid statements such as...

"I have all the money in the world to myself."

Isn't that a little greedy? Why wouldn't you want other people to have money?

Maybe you would like to have your own foundation and use money to help people.

"I have way more money than I'll ever need for myself. Now I have my foundation in place and I'm helping people. I always have more than enough money for myself but the more I give away through my foundation and help others, more money comes back to me and I put it into my foundation."

Maybe you have trouble imagining money "just coming to you" (if so, again you're trying to be rational when your Subconscious Mind is ir-rational). It can come to you in many ways.

You could stumble upon something that's very valuable. You hear on the news at times when people come across something that's worth a lot of money.

Around the turn of this century I heard on the news that a fellow bought a painting at either an antique or pawn shop. He only wanted the frame.

When he got home and removed the painting, he found a copy of either – I can't remember which -- the Constitution or the Declaration of Independence. He took it to (I believe) the Library of Congress where it was verified to be an original document hand written by our Founding Fathers. He was given $1 million for it.

I'm not suggesting he used his Mind Power to find it. I don't know if he did. I'm suggesting that things like that happen. You can cause them to happen with your Mind Power. You could do an affirmation this way...

"Wherever I go I always find something that is of great value moneywise. Like this rare gold coin I found that is worth a tremendous amount of money (then imagine you're looking at a rare gold coin you're holding in the palm of your hand. If you don't know what one looks like, just imagine it or get a picture of one.) *I'm always stumbling on to things that are worth huge sums of money. They follow me around wherever I go."*

As I say, you can <u>TRY</u> it that way for awhile to see if that works, but I think it's best to not force the situation in which you get money. Allow your Subconscious Mind and the Universe to find their own ways to get it to you.

Here's another way you can try this if you're self employed or have your own business in which having more clients or customers means more income.

The late, great motivational speaker Zig Ziglar said...

"You can have anything you want if you help enough people get what they want."

You can affirm...

"I'm helping so many people with my business (or service or practice). *Clients* (or customers) *come to me in droves. More and more clients* (or

customers) *come to me all the time. It's such a great feeling to help more and more people with my service* (or business or practice). *I've established myself as THE expert in my field...not for ego's sake, but it means I'm helping more people who need my service* (or practice or business) *than anyone else has. I attract clients* (or customers) *to me in avalanches. And people are happy to pay me whatever I charge for my service* (or products) *because it helps them so much."*

Notice in all the affirmations of this section I didn't mention a dollar amount. I didn't affirm...

"I have a million dollars"...

because that's a finite amount of money **(<u>Key #4</u> – The Subconscious Mind only thinks in infinite or absolute terms).**

As I mentioned earlier, don't put too much effort into this. Just do a good 15-20 minute affirmation session following the relaxation in the morning, then forget about it the rest of the day. Try that for several weeks or a month. Too much effort may get in the way. If you don't see results in several weeks or a month you can try a second affirmation in the evening.

And again, this could show you how easy it is to train your Subconscious Mind to give you what you want. But after doing the affirmation, don't go back to worrying about money concerns...bills, not having enough, etc.

I know it's easy to worry about not having enough money, especially if you have a family and the economy is in a down turn. Perhaps your job is in jeopardy. That's all the more reason to stop worrying about money and affirm you have enough of it.

You may be in the habit of worrying about money. If so, it became a habit because you worried a lot. But just as you got in the habit of worrying about money, you can get in the habit of *<u>feeling</u>* you have a lot of money.

It takes effort and a constant reminder to think and feel the right way, to break that old habit. You have to change the way you think. If you start to worry about money, right at that moment start to think and *feel* that you have it. Start to say some of the lines from your affirmation. If you continue to think the same way, you'll continue to get the same thing.

Attracting Possessions

If you would love to have something and look at the price tag, don't ever say…

"I can't afford it."

Let's say you want a car, and you love Corvettes. Imagine you have one and are driving it.

"I love my new Vette. I love the smooth ride. I love this black leather interior, and the black (or whatever color) *shine that comes off the body's finish. Look at that dashboard…that looks cool"* (then imagine you're looking at the dash board…the speedometer and tachometer are going wild. Look at the black leather and the shine that comes off of it).

Imagine you're driving it, feeling the vibration, hearing the engine while driving down an open highway 100 miles an hour, and feeling the happy feelings you would get from owning and driving it. Imagine you have the stereo blasting with your favorite music…imagine you're seeing every detail you would want in it.

So how would this get you the car of your dreams that you can't afford (ouch!!! Don't say that)? If after doing the affirmation EVERY DAY without ever doubting it will happen, you won't walk out to your driveway one day and PUFF…like magic there's your new car. Rather, things will start to go your way enabling you to get it. Your Subconscious Mind will find a way for you to get it.

Let's say after several weeks, or maybe a month of doing the affirmation you go to work and your boss calls you into his/her office. You learn that a colleague has put in their notice to take a new job, and your boss wants you to fill that open position. And it's a promotion, with a nice salary increase. What can you do with the raise? HELLO!!! You can afford the car now.

That's one way it could happen. If that's how it happens, you could rationalize it -- and believe less in Your Power -- by saying...

"*He/she* (your colleague) *got a new job and that allowed me to afford the car by getting that promotion. I didn't have anything to do with it.*"

Ahhhh, could it be that by using your Mind Power you influenced the boss' decision at the other company -- without him/her knowing it – to hire your colleague making their position available, and you also influenced your boss' decision without him/her consciously knowing it to promote you and not another colleague? I'll explain this aspect later.

Attracting A Soul Mate

If you've found your soul mate and you two are together, then congratulations. But if not, you can find him/her this way.

Imagine he/she looks exactly the way you want him/her to look, having the personality, characteristics and qualities you want. Think of everything you would want your soul mate to be, and then imagine you're together. Imagine you're saying to each other...

"I'm so glad we found each other. I love you. We're lovers for eternity. I don't want anyone else but you. You're my soul mate. I can feel it down to the very depths of my being."

Feel his/her arms around you as you embrace. Imagine you go everywhere with each other (if that's what you want).

Even if you don't have any requirements about looks, personality or qualities, you can still attract a soul mate.

"I'm sooo glad I've found my soul mate. He/she is everything I always wanted in a man/woman. And he/she loves me as much as I love him/her. I couldn't have asked for anything more in a man/woman."

What if you've found your soul mate but s/he doesn't love you? I address this issue later on.

Curing Disease

I am in no way suggesting you never go to the doctor, or skip having regular exams. Get those mammograms, colonoscopies, lipid profiles, yearly physicals, etc. And follow your doctor's advice if a problem is detected. But you can incorporate Your Power into the regimen to fix any problems quicker. Remember the cancerous brain tumor example?

"Oh, I'm soooo happy that the tumor in my brain has dissolved away. I'm soooo happy that I'm cured...now I'm free of cancer. I have a new lease on life. It's soooo great to be cured of that cancerous tumor that was in my brain."

Be very specific. Say the name of the disease and where it is in the body. Focus like a laser beam on them. You can affirm generalities, such as...

"I am perfect health. My body radiates perfect health."

But don't make them the thrust of what you affirm.

Concentrate on the areas of your body that you want cured. Remember the light of relaxation?

"The Light of Healing is shining on that tumor in my brain and has dissolved the tumor away. Now I radiate perfect health."

Now, in this situation you're trying to get rid of something. When dealing with a serious illness you can't use your Mind Power too much. Do at least several 15-20 minute affirmation sessions a day. The more the better. Affirm it all day long. Keep thinking and ***feeling*** those happy thoughts of being cured throughout the day. Pretend you're cured. Trick your Subconscious Mind into thinking you're cured.

And if your doctor prescribes treatments do what you're told. But DO NOT start to worry about having the illness. If you do, start to say lines from the affirmation.

Now, do the same for any disease you have. Just change its name.

Preventing Disease

You've heard the saying…

"an ounce of prevention is worth a pound of cure."

I do this once a week to prevent disease.

I sit down and do the relaxation. I see "The Light of Relaxation" as "The Light of Healing". I start in my brain.

"The light of healing is shining deeply into my brain and has dissolved away any tumors that had developed. There are no tumors anywhere in my brain. It's impossible for me to get any tumors because I am immune to cancer and all diseases. Now, the light of healing is shining deeply into the blood vessels in my brain and has washed away any plaque that had developed. My blood vessels are totally clear and wide open. Blood flows through them so effortlessly. My blood vessels are completely healthy and strong. It's impossible for me to have an aneurysm…it's impossible for my

blood vessels to burst open…they're so strong. It's impossible for me to get a stroke because the platelets in my blood cannot stick together to form a clot, so I can never have a stroke. The platelets in my blood stay as far away from each other as they can. They repel each other."

Then I move that light of healing all the way down to my toes, having it shine on every organ…my tongue and insides of my mouth (to prevent oral cancer), my throat, lungs, heart including cholesterol (*"my HDL, LDL and Triglycerides are at their most healthful levels"*), arteries to the heart (*"the light of healing has dissolved away any plaque that was in my arteries. The blood flows through the arteries to my heart so effortlessly"*), stomach, pancreas, gall bladder, kidneys, liver, colon, rectum, testicles, prostate, all the way down the arteries of my legs (too much plaque in them can cause arterial peripheral disease – heart disease), then bones (*"they're healthy and strong and cancer free. It's impossible for them to weaken or develop osteoporosis"*), then all down my skin from head to toe to prevent skin cancer.

I spend about a minute or two on each body part. It takes me 30 to 40 minutes. If you don't want to take that much time at once, you can do the upper half of your body one day, the lower half the next.

If you're new at harnessing Your Power, you might want to do that exercise every day for several weeks to a month, then maybe a few days a week for a month, then one day a week after that.

"Scary" Disease Prevention

It seems we often hear about new and scary diseases breaking out. What makes them scary is that many times there are no known treatments for them...no known effective antibiotics. And a new vaccine has to be created.

Remember the November 2002 outbreak of SARS (Severe Acute Respiratory Syndrome)? The World Health Organization says it began in southern China resulting in 8,098 cases with 774 deaths reported in 37 countries...the majority in China and Hong Kong. No cases have been reported since 2004.

Instead of being worried about a new, scary disease when news of it breaks – fearing you might contract it – use Your Power to prevent it in addition to what your doctor advises.

"I have the strongest immune system ever created. I am immune to this new disease. It's impossible for me to come down with it. If it enters my body my immune system sees it immediately and destroys it. There's a protective shield all around my body preventing all disease from entering. I am immune to all disease. Its impossible for me to get sick."

And remember...thousands of people die every year from the flu. So use Your Power to prevent it.

Speaking of antibiotics, many in the medical community believe they're being used so much now that society is building an immunity to them thereby reducing their effectiveness. That should give you more incentive to use Your Power to keep you from getting diseases.

Staying Safe

You don't need me to tell you that accidents happen. In fact the Centers For Disease Control has said for years that accidents are the leading cause of death for people under the age of 65. But you can use Your Power to help reduce your chances of being an accident victim.

Every so often you can affirm…

"I'm so glad I'm always safe. Wherever I go, wherever I am and however I get there I am always safe. I always arrive safely at destinations. I'm always safe in whatever location I find myself. I'm so happy to be out and about whenever I can knowing I am always safe and return home safely."

You can do this affirmation separately from time to time, or include it if you use Your Power to stay free of disease.

Eliminating Allergies

Do you have allergies of any kind? Use your Mind Power to get rid of them. Let's say you have allergies to pollen. Don't start to do this when your allergies flare up. It might be harder to get rid of the symptoms then. But about a month before the pollen season you can affirm…

"I'm soooo glad I no longer have an allergy to pollen. It feels so great to not break out during pollen season. Look! Pollen is falling all over me but I don't have any bad reaction to it. There's pollen on my head, on my face and all over my body but I have no reaction to it all. I'm not sneezing at all. That's because I am no longer allergic to pollen. Wow, it's sooo great to have gotten rid of that allergy."

***Caution*: Do not try that with an allergy that could kill you if eaten (such as peanuts) or if contact with it is made, then eat it or come in contact with it to see if you're no longer allergic. Do the affirmation and then have your doctor run tests on you to determine that you're no longer allergic.**

Quick Healing From Injuries

Getting injured is certainly no fun. But you can get over them more quickly by using Your Power in addition to the natural healing process.

Let's say you sprained an ankle and need to be on crutches for a while:

"My ankle is completely healed from its sprain. The Light Of Healing is shining deeply into my ankle and has healed it completely. The sprain is gone and so is the pain. I can now walk pain free with no crutches. I'm so glad my ankle has completely healed."

In Conclusion

So there are just SOME examples of using Your Power to get what you want. Whenever you have ANYTHING in your life you want or that needs to be resolved, improved or eliminated...use your Mind Power. You're only limited to how much you can use it by how limited you think it is.

And remember...a good 15-20 minutes a session. That's what takes Mind Power beyond Positive Thinking. But you'll see that the more you use your power the shorter the affirmation sessions need to be. In an upcoming chapter you'll learn how I got My Power to work very quickly...IN SECONDS!

So in this chapter we talked about getting just about anything you want. But what about getting what you...*don't* want?

Huh? What?

CHAPTER 8

Getting What You DON'T Want

Did this chapter's title throw you off a bit? Why would you try to get something you don't want?

For one reason, when people get married and have children, they quickly learn – if they're responsible adults, that is – that their lives aren't about them anymore…it's about their children. And there are things they know they MUST NOT DO…including things they enjoy.

They come to realize they have to drop bad habits so they don't set bad examples for their kids. They may have to give up drinking too much alcohol or doing illegal drugs, or stop smoking cigarettes or lose weight and live a healthy lifestyle so their kids do the same when they get married and have their own children.

Even single people can come to those realizations and know they have to drop bad habits for their own good. But if they don't have children they have an easier "out" than parents. They don't want to give up things that give them pleasure…even when they know they're doing them harm in the long run. The thought of giving those things up turns them off. So it may be even harder for them to "get around to it" than it is for parents.

And that's where the mind game struggle comes in…"the thought" of having to give up something they like. They have programmed their

Subconscious to believe they don't want to give up those activities. So they fight with themselves about getting around to it.

If you find yourself in that situation, you may never get around to it if you keep telling yourself things such as...

"*but I don't want to give up drinking alcohol, or smoking cigarettes or pot, or spending too much money on pornography or gambling, or giving up fatty foods I like in order to lose weight*", etc., etc.

You're programming your Subconscious with thoughts of...

"*I don't want to.*"

So if you know you need to make important changes in your life but can't get started because you don't want to give up something you enjoy, change your attitude by programming your Subconscious with thoughts of...

"*I want to.*"

To help you in your effort, here is...

An Introduction To Self-Hypnosis

Because of Hollywood, Hypnosis is a very misunderstood medium. I have never seen a movie or television show (comedy or drama) that depicted the process accurately. I'm not saying there has never been any. I haven't seen them. I've seen documentaries that have. But documentaries don't have that "Hollywood flare" and are supposed to be factually correct.

Hypnotists cannot put subjects "under their spell", or make subjects do anything they don't want to do. When a subject does what a hypnotist tells them to do, it's because the subject wants to do it. Therefore, all hypnosis is self-hypnosis. The subject is allowing themselves to be hypnotized by following the direction of the hypnotist's suggestions.

A hypnotist cannot put a subject in a trance that only the hypnotist can break. The subject can come out of it whenever s/he wants. And what a subject "comes out of" is nothing more than a deep state of relaxation.

When you're "hypnotized" you're conscious, alert and very aware of your surroundings. You're in control of the situation. While you can get to different levels of consciousness when your mind is very relaxed you're not in some other *state* of mind that only hypnosis can get you to.

Hypnosis is not mind control or brainwashing. It's merely a process in which a person plants suggestions in their Subconscious Mind while in a relaxed state. It is ***NOTHING*** more than that.

Now, it may seem that I've oversimplified what hypnosis is. But so far I've only explained the process. What makes hypnosis a valuable tool in helping people resolve relationship problems with their spouse or children or whatever issues that are disrupting their lives depends on the expertise of the hypnotherapist. An experienced one knows what questions to ask a subject, how to guide them so they can see for themselves what those issues are...the roots of which are embedded in the subconscious mind. And when a subject can *consciously* see those roots for themselves, that's usually all it takes for them to "let them go" and be freed of them.

That's why – in my opinion – hypnotherapy conducted by an experienced hypnotherapist – brings about quicker relief for clients because it's conducted on a subconscious level where as psychotherapy is conducted on the conscious level.

Breaking Addictions

Hypnotherapists treat people with addictions all the time. I saw a man on television who used hypnotherapy to quit smoking cigarettes. He said...

"I don't know what the hypnotherapist did, but it worked."

I've been telling you all along what a hypnotherapist does. If you use your Subconscious Mind to get what you want you would be the self-hypnotherapist. It's the same process I've been showing you...program the Subconscious Mind for whatever you want by planting suggestions into it while in a deep state of relaxation just as a hypnotherapist would do for you.

So if you're trying to quit smoking, here's a way to quit by using Your Mind Power.

"Boy, I am soooo glad I quit smoking. When I smoke, it makes me really sick and I hate the taste of it. Uggghh. Just thinking of sticking another cigarette in my mouth and inhaling all that tar and nicotine makes me want to throw up (imagine how you feel just before you throw up). *I'm sooo glad all the tar and nicotine are out of my system and that I have no urge to smoke. Every last molecule of tar and nicotine has left my system. The urge to smoke has completely gone away."*

Imagine you're inhaling a drag and it makes you sick...feel like you're sick, imagine you're sick. Cough vigorously.

You might want to try a 15-20 minute affirmation session just claiming how all the tar and nicotine are out of your system as a way to get unhooked.

Just as you would want to feel the positive emotions while doing affirmations to get something you want, feel the negative emotions you would feel if smoking made you sick. Then, feel happy that you gave up the habit.

Continue to smoke if you must when you start in with this and see if your urge to smoke dwindles over time, down to zero.

Do you have other addictions you want to break? Use the affirmation I used for this section and change the words to fit the addiction.

Weight Loss

Do you have a weight problem? Have you wanted to lose weight for some time but can't get around to it? The thought of giving up food you enjoy that keeps the extra pounds on prevents you from starting?

Use self-hypnosis/affirmations to get you going.

"I'm so glad I started the weight loss program. It was easier to get started than I thought it would be. Now, I no longer crave all those foods (mention them specifically here) *that keep those extra pounds on me. I have no desire to eat them. I enjoy eating healthy. I'm now down to the weight I'm supposed to be. I love the way I look now* (imagine you're looking at yourself in a mirror naked and seeing yourself with a slim body)*. My metabolism is extremely fast. It burns every excess pound of fat sooo quickly."*

Do that for a while before you start a weight loss program and see how your attitude towards weight loss changes. You'll have a positive attitude toward it. Chances of succeeding will be much greater than if you entered such a program with a negative attitude by saying something such as...

"Oh, I can't get into dieting."

Try to start a weight loss program with that attitude and you won't get very far. You can't get into changing your diet to lose weight because you've already convinced your Subconscious Mind that you can't or don't want to. Now, just convince it that you enjoy eating healthy to lose weight.

I read an article in which the author informed readers of using the Subconscious Mind to help them with weight loss. She said to start with "realistic" goals. If you're a woman size 20 and want to get down to a size 6, it's a more "realistic" goal to see yourself at a size 18 than 6. So say affirmations stating and visualizing yourself a size 18. Then when you get to that size, say affirmations stating you're size 16, then 14, then 12, etc. etc. until you get to size 6.

What have I been saying all along? **Key #6 – The Subconscious Mind is your il-logical/ ir-rational mind.**

Your Subconscious Mind does not think "realistically" as your conscious mind does. You can say affirmations as the author of that article suggested. It will just take longer to achieve your goal.

Affirm you have the body you want NOW. You'll achieve your goal much quicker. Your Subconscious Mind will not think…

"Wow, you're a size 20 and want to be a size 6? Gee, it's not realistic to think that. I can get you to a size 18 because that's a more realistic goal. But I don't know about size 6 right now. Maybe eventually I can get you there."

Plus, don't think in sizes. **Key #4 – The Subconscious Mind only thinks in infinite or absolute terms.**

Size 18, size 16, size 14…those are finite terms. Just picture yourself with the body you want, or affirm…

"All the excess body fat that made me overweight is gone."

"All" is an absolute term or idea. Does doing it my way mean you say the affirmation 15-20 minutes one day and the next day all the excess weight is gone? Of course not. But saying the affirmation every day while losing weight will get you to your goal much faster.

Fitness

Most of us know the importance of exercise. Does that mean most of us exercise? Of course not. But even if you don't exercise you don't need me to tell you that it's one of the keys to living a long and healthy life. Study after study has proven that.

It's a fact that we're living longer. But while the quantity of life has increased, the quality has not. I think that because we continue to live longer, the quality of life in our older years has decreased. I see so many people as young as their 60's with many health problems. What fun is it to live a long life if you can't enjoy your later years because of ill health, weak bones and joints, osteoporosis, heart disease and everything else that makes it a struggle just to get around? The sad part about it is, most of it can be avoided...or at least greatly minimized.

In his book ***"Ageless Body, Timeless Mind"***, Dr. Deepak Chopra says the human body is a machine that can actually get ***stronger*** as it gets older. I agree. But that can only happen with exercise. You have to make the body strong and then keep it strong into and throughout your senior years. If you don't, the body will only weaken over time.

Cardiovascular exercise is important, but that by itself won't make your body stronger. Since we have a muscular-skeletal system in addition to a cardiovascular system, you also need some type of weight or resistance training to make the muscles strong and your joints flexible so you can keep them strong and flexible into and throughout your older years.

You don't have to go into a gym trying to look like Mr./Ms. Olympia when you're a senior citizen (although that is possible. The great Albert Beckles competed as a professional bodybuilder into his 60's. That proves that you can keep your body strong into and throughout your senior years). All you have to do is put enough resistance to your muscles to challenge them and keep them strong.

Dr. Chopra also says one reason we age and experience its negative effects – more aches and pains, for instance – is because we expect it. We've conditioned our minds to accept the fact that we age and will experience more aches and pains and other health problems as we get older. We see it as a natural state of affairs. We take it for granted that it happens.

We've programmed our Subconscious Mind in a negative way. But you can condition your Subconscious Mind that you don't age.

Does that mean you can stop the aging process? No. But you can greatly slow it down so that you prevent – or at least -- minimize those aches and pains, provided you exercise the cardiovascular and muscular-skeletal systems regularly.

Of course it's never too late to start an exercise program. But it's best to make your body strong before your senior years. Then, maintaining it through those years will be easy…a lot easier than trying to make your body fit once you reach your senior years.

Think about it. You'll spend your entire adult life planning for retirement… the time when you're supposed to really enjoy life to the fullest. You'll put money away to travel, take up hobbies you didn't have time for when you were working. There'll be places to go and people to see.

But when the time finally arrives, you can't do those things because of health problems that could have been avoided or minimized if you had exercised and taken care of your body before then.

If you're convinced now of the importance of exercising but you still can't make the effort for whatever reason…

"*I don't have the time*", or "*I can't get into exercising*"...

trick your Subconscious Mind into believing you enjoy exercising.

"I'm sooo glad I took up exercise. I feel so much better since I started. I really enjoy it. I can always find the time to do it. I love the fact that I've made

my body healthy and strong and will keep it that way into my senior years. I really enjoy exercising and look forward to it. The thought of missing an exercise session really bothers me. I can't even think of missing a session. It has become such a part of my routine now. I'm sooo glad I got into exercising. I love doing my cardio and strength training routines. I have made both my cardiovascular and muscular-skeletal systems very strong."

Try a 15-20 minute affirmation session every morning before you start an exercise routine. See what happens in a few weeks.

You may be thinking...

"*couldn't I just imagine I'm exercising and benefit that way?*"

Theoretically, you could. There are studies showing that people imagined they were dieting and exercising and lost weight and built muscle. You might want to wait until your Mind Power becomes a bit more advanced before you try it. If you try it early on in your development and it doesn't work you may become discouraged and give up trying to develop your power all together.

I've never tried it myself. I enjoy the real thing...going to the gym, hearing the weights clang and sweating from pumping iron or doing my cardio workout...then hitting the shower.

What Are Your Goals And Desires?

I've given you many examples as to how you can use Your Mind Power to get just about anything you want...and how to make it easier for you to do things you don't want to do but know you MUST. And I could go on and on giving you examples. But by now you should have a good idea as to how the Subconscious Mind works and how you can apply it to help you attain just about any desire you have.

I tried to show you in these two chapters what I meant in the Introduction…that this book is the only one you need.

When you want to improve your life in ANY way – whether it's attaining something, ridding yourself of something such as disease or addictions, having to do something you don't want to do but know you must, or whatever it is you're trying to do to create the life of your dreams -- write an affirmation claiming you have it NOW. Trick the Subconscious Mind into believing you have it NOW and that you no longer hate things you MUST do for your own good. Make sure your affirmation follows **"The 6 Keys"** and you'll have all your bases covered.

CHAPTER 9

Let Us Pray...But Not That Way

*(**Note:** If you're not religious or spiritual you can skip this section if you'd like, although I would like you to read it. You can be an atheist and still develop Your Power. Simply leave out any reference to God while saying affirmations.)*

I remember in 2007 hearing a story on ABC News with Charles Gibson about a study that concluded the use of prayer to cure disease had been shown to *not* be very effective. It didn't surprise me because ***people don't pray correctly***!

People who are religious and pray often would pray this way in trying to heal themselves of disease:

"Oh Dear God, please cure me of this cancer. Please use your Infinite Power to take this cancer from me. Please make me well again, Dear God."

What's wrong with that prayer? Is it stated in the present? No, in the future. It's asking for something that *PRESENTLY* hasn't happened.

Plus, remember about feeling the emotions you would feel if you had what you wanted? What emotions would a person feel if praying in such a way? Doubt, fear, maybe anger and pity. They wouldn't feel joyous about being cancer free.

I've heard many religious and spiritual leaders say the purpose of prayer is to give thanks, not to ask for something. So here's how to pray correctly.

"*Oh, Dear God, thank you for curing me of cancer. Thank you for using your Infinite Power to dissolve that cancerous tumor from my brain. That tumor in my brain is gone now, thanks to you Dear God.*"

Remember that Light of Relaxation?

"*Thank you God for shining your Light of Healing onto that tumor in my brain. Your Light of Healing shines continuously on the spot where that tumor used to be and has dissolved it away. The tumor in my brain has gone.*"

Do you see how easier it would be to imagine those happy feelings of being cured if you pray that way instead of asking God to heal you?

You may have heard this before. Someone tells a friend…

"I prayed and prayed but God didn't answer my prayers."

Then the friend says…

"He answered your prayers. He said 'No.'"

God never says "No". But He won't answer your prayers if you ask Him for something in the future.

Who was it who said…

"Ask and it shall be given unto you"?

That's not quite correct. It's…

"Feel that you have it NOW, act like you have it NOW, thank God for giving it to you NOW, THEN it will be given unto you."

Do you know "The Lord's Prayer"? This is how it and all prayers should be stated:

"Our father who art in Heaven, hallowed IS thy name. Thy kingdom HAS come, Thy will HAS BEEN done on earth as it is in Heaven. THANK YOU for giving us this day our daily bread. And THANK YOU for forgiving our trespasses as we HAVE FORGIVEN those who have trespassed against us. And THANK YOU for not leading us into temptation and FOR DELIVERING us from evil. For thine is the kingdom, the power and the glory forever and ever. Amen."

Just as your Subconscious Mind is il-logical/ir-rational so too is God. He is infinite, which means no beginning and no end. How can something that exists have no beginning? That's not logical, is it?

And just as your Subconscious Mind only thinks in the present, so too does God. Many orders of Christianity (and perhaps other faiths as well) say a thousand years to us may only seem like one day to God.

You can't even say it that way because one day is a finite period of time, and God doesn't think in finite terms because He's infinite. He only thinks and sees NOW. Therefore, God sees everything that happened in the past, everything that's happening in the present, and everything that's going to happen in the future as if it's all happening NOW.

That doesn't make logical sense either, does it?

We don't have a spirit and a Subconscious Mind. Your Subconscious Mind *IS* your Spirit, which is *GOD'S* Spirit while at the same time your Spirit *IS* your Subconscious Mind. They are one in the same. That's why the Subconscious Mind is so powerful. We have the power of God within us.

Your Subconscious Mind/Your Spirit -- God's Spirit -- was with you at the moment you were conceived. How does a fetus know how to develop? It needs the right information. And what is the only Thing that knows that information?

But is God logical or rational? No. He's il-logical/ir-rational.

Perhaps you'll understand it easier this way. Have you ever had a dream that came true? It's a very common experience. A few weeks before my father passed away I dreamed that he had died. He wasn't in ill health at the time I had the dream. So his death was not something that was pending in the family's mind. And the scenario surrounding his passing was exactly the way I dreamed it.

When you dream about something that comes true, your Subconscious Mind sees how God sees…it's seeing a future event happening NOW.

When you dream about something that happened in the past your Subconscious Mind sees it happening NOW.

Can that mean...could it possibly be, we are God?

CHAPTER 10

Get Off That Couch!

I saw an interview by Mike Wallace on "60 Minutes" with singer/ actress Barbra Streisand. He asked why she had to be in therapy with psychologists for 30 years. She said…

"I'm a slow learner."

I'll comment on that interview more in a moment.

This chapter will be very beneficial if you're not a victim of *"The Unwritten Universal Law"*, but you've had problems in your life due to a negative upbringing causing you to have low self esteem and thoughts of being a loser. Or maybe you were bullied a lot as a kid and others made fun of you making you feel isolated from the world.

While most people think of using their Subconscious Mind to attract what they want -- to build a life of success or happiness or whatever else they're trying to attain, or to use it to cure themselves of disease and to prevent disease – our Mind Power can also help people deal with situations that prompt many to seek help from traditional therapists. That can include issues such as low self esteem, grief over the death of a friend or loved one, loneliness, fears or phobia. If a person needs medication to treat a psychotic disorder then a psychiatrist – being a Medical Doctor – needs to be sought. Only such a professional can prescribe medication.

Now, before we continue…I want to say that I am only speaking of my experiences as they relate to me. I am in no way advising anyone as to what they should or shouldn't do. I'm only offering suggestions as to what options are available if you need help in dealing with a psychological or emotional situation that's not of a medical disorder.

One thing I tried in order to find out what was making me a loser so I could end my life of struggling was spending 18 years in and out of traditional therapy. And for me, that was almost a total waste of time and money. Insurance covered 80 percent of it. Having to pay 20 percent at each session didn't break me, but over 18 years it added up to a lot.

But it was a learning experience. I learned that while many people have been helped with traditional therapy, others are in it for years without ever being "cured". I came to learn after all those years – *FROM MY EXPERIENCE* – that going to someone week to week, sitting and talking to them, trying to understand my situation on a conscious/intellectual level never healed me. It did nothing to end my struggles…or even help me discover what was causing them.

Let me give you an example as to why I say that. One night I caught the last 20 minutes of a documentary on traditional therapy. There was an interview at the very end with a man who had been under a therapist's care for being a "flasher". He couldn't control an urge to open his overcoat and expose his private parts to people…mostly women. You couldn't make out his identity because he was silhouetted during the interview.

I remember him saying...

"It's getting better. I'm learning to control my urges more, but I know… it's going to be one day at a time."

When I heard that I thought…

"that guy is going to spend the rest of his life dealing with his urges, having to work constantly at controlling them, will probably have some relapses along the way. And it's going to be a life long struggle for him."

If his therapy had been conducted on a subconscious level by using his Mind Power to go into his Subconscious Mind and discover what was the programming or issue in his psyche that was causing him to be a flasher and then had used his Mind Power to get rid of it, the issue would have been removed, his urges would have stopped and he would have ended his flasher ways. In essence, he would have been... "cured".

But by having his therapy conducted on an intellectual level solely from within the conscious mind, getting him to understand his actions and learning to control his urges, he never discovers WHY he's a flasher. The issue never gets removed from his psyche and he has to fight with his urges the rest of his life... "one day at a time" as he said.

Grief Relief

Grief counseling is one issue handled by some type of therapist. I've never needed professional help for that issue. But I can tell you if it's conducted on a conscious level in which the therapist talks to the client for an hour or so once a week, helping them to understand their grief intellectually...it's going to take more than one session to resolve it. Most likely, only TIME will help the client finally feel relief.

But I helped a cousin resolve an extreme case of grief in 20 minutes by using her Mind Power. I called her one day to see how she was doing following her mother's death. She said she was having a very difficult time, was dealing with a huge amount of grief and a feeling of loss she couldn't shake.

She told me that at her father's funeral her mother said she wanted to go live with her husband and be with him forever in Heaven. And that gave me the idea for an affirmation for her to say. Without telling her I instructed her to use her Mind Power.

I told her to get her body relaxed, and then say over and over for a good 15-20 minutes…

"*I'm so glad that Mom is with Dad now. I'm so happy they're together once again. That's exactly what Mom wanted. They're together now, eternally happy living in Paradise…I'm just so happy for her and Dad.*"

I told her to feel happy while saying it…to feel so happy that Mom finally got her wish and was with her husband again…to feel happy for her mother and father...to picture them as angels the way they are always pictured wearing angel clothing and halos, hugging and smiling at each other.

I called her the next day because she was going to come to my house for more coaching. But she said…

"*Hey Todd, I don't have to come see you because yesterday I did what you told me to do and I woke up this morning feeling really good. I actually feel happy. I feel so relieved, like the grief is out of me.*"

Bingo!!!! Just one 20-minute Mind Power session was all it took. I did instruct her that if she feels the grief coming back -- which is very common for when someone experiences such a huge loss – it shouldn't be as strong as it was at first. And that she could do the Mind Power session again… and whenever she felt the grief coming on. Time needed for the sessions would happen further and further apart until it was gone for good.

I could have counseled her by helping her understand her grief by saying something such as…

"*You must understand…death is a part of the life process. Life comes to an end for everyone. If you can understand that you should be able to eventually let go of your grief. Just give it some time.*"

Ahhh…I think being an adult she already knew that. But re-enforcing it on a conscious level would not have helped rid herself of grief. ONLY when she went into her Subconscious Mind and replaced her feeling of loss with the feeling of happiness that her Mother and Father "are together again in Paradise" did her feeling of grief wash away.

Why did that work? **Key #2 – The Subconscious Mind does not know the difference between what is real, and what you imagine to be real.**

She imagined a happy scenario in her Subconscious to replace her unhappy emotions with happy ones.

There are other ways to formulate your affirmations to relieve yourself of the grief when a loved one passes. How do we try to console others who've lost a loved one? We say to them...

"Be happy that (name) *is in a better place now."*

If you've lost a loved one imagine for a good 15-20 minutes that you're seeing him/her in Heaven and they are so happy being with friends while telling yourself…

"I'm so happy that (name) *is in a better place now enjoying their everlasting life in paradise. S/he looks so happy being with others. I'm so happy for him/her."*

If the loved one was sick for a very long time or was born with severe handicaps that made their life a struggle…

"I'm so happy (name) *has found relief and is no longer suffering. S/he looks so happy now. S/he has finally found peace and happiness."*

And in all of those Mind Power sessions, feel happy for the person while doing the visualization. Put a smile on your face. Imagine those happy feelings. Replace the feelings of loss and grief with feelings of happiness for the loved one who's now gone. They're now in "a better place". Do that whenever the grief resurfaces. It will reduce its severity and frequency.

Rewriting History

It's been said that you can't rewrite history. But you can…in your Subconscious Mind.

I've gone to some of the self help and self improvement forums on the internet. I'm amazed and saddened to read of all the baggage people are carrying from relationships they had with their parents when they were children and teenagers and how it's still bogging them down.

If you're carrying such baggage you can get rid of it, you can make peace with your parents even if they're deceased or if they haven't tried to make peace with you.

I'll use this example as an illustration. I remember seeing the actor Kirk Douglas on television. He said when he was a kid his father never told him he was proud of him, never gave him a pat on the back and said…

"*Atta boy. Way to go. I'm proud of you.*"

But he said his father could tell other people he was proud of him.

If that's a similar situation for you and it's still negatively affecting you because you felt it was something you needed as a child and didn't get, use Your Power.

Do the relaxation for about five minutes, then imagine you're with your father and he's telling you how proud of you he is, that he's praising you. Think of a situation when you were a child and you were looking to him for adulation but didn't get it. Imagine that situation is playing out the way you wanted it to.

Important: Imagine you are that child, not the adult you are now.

Imagine feeling his hand when he pats you on the back. Look at his face when he tells you he's proud of you. See him smiling, pretend you're hugging each other and feel the sensation of his arms around you. Imagine you're telling each other...

"I love you."

Do that for a good 15-20 minutes, just as you would say an affirmation.

Why does this work? Once again, **Key #2 – The Subconscious Mind does not know the difference between what is real and what is imagined.**

Your Subconscious Mind believes you're finally getting what you wanted.

And...**The Subconscious Mind only thinks in the present (Key #1).** It will see you as presently getting what you wanted even though you'll be playing out in your mind a situation that happened years ago. Your Subconscious Mind still sees that situation as *presently* happening and now sees you *presently* getting what you want.

So sit down with paper and a pen or pencil and write down every situation you can remember when one or both of your parents didn't give you what you wanted from them emotionally, or acted toward you in a way that emotionally harmed you.

Did they belittle you in front of friends, or told you that you were pathetic after you made mistakes, or yelled at you for things you felt weren't your fault, or never told you they loved you? Try to think of as many situations as you can...those that are still negatively affecting you today.

Also, try this with situations that at the time harmed you but you don't consciously feel their harmful affects now. They may still be affecting you subconsciously.

Imagine those situations are playing out the way you wanted them to. Take one situation at a time. Do the visualization over several days for 15-20 minutes. Imagine your parent's are acting the way you wanted them to.

Also, if your parents yelled at you a lot or embarrassed you in front of friends, or emotionally harmed you in any other way...imagine he/she is apologizing to you for the way they acted.

Again, imagine you're that little kid. Hear him/her saying...

"I understand now what I said/did made you feel badly. I'm sorry."

This will validate your feelings, which every child needs. You'll finally be getting what you wanted and needed. It may not relieve your hurtful emotions permanently after one or two sessions, but when you feel the harmful effects resurfacing, you can keep them at bay by doing the visualization again every morning for several days.

Over time, you'll notice the resurfacing of those bad feelings and their negative effects on you are occurring further and further apart, and to a lesser degree.

You can also do this with friends or acquaintances. Let's say a good friend doesn't want to see you anymore because s/he thought you said something negative about them to someone else when you didn't and you want to explain the situation to them. But they don't want to talk to you ever again and you can't reach them to apologize or explain what really happened so you can patch things up.

You can imagine you're talking with him/her and saying you're sorry or explaining to them it wasn't you who said "that thing about them" to others. Hear him/her forgive you and imagine you're shaking hands or hugging each other and are good friends again. Even if you never get to see them again, that can help you eliminate the guilt.

Healing Your Inner Child

You may have heard of "The Inner Child" concept. It is definitely valid. That's because **Key #1** – the Subconscious only thinks in the present. It forever sees everything that happens to us – even things that happened when we're children – as still happening NOW.

When we're little children before our conscious minds form, we only have a Subconscious Mind which – as I informed you in **Key #6** – is our ir-rational mind. As very young children, we're irrational people. We become more rational as we grow older and our rational, conscious mind further develops.

You've probably heard the saying...

"Time heals all wounds."

That's true for emotional wounds we experience as rational adults because we understand life better than young children do. We know things can go wrong at times...even if we don't understand why.

But if emotional wounds we experience as irrational children don't heal by releasing their hurtful effects from our psyche, time can make those wounds – and the harm they cause us – get worse.

This brings me back to the interview with Barbra Streisand. The only reason she gave for being in therapy when Mike Wallace asked her was...

"My mother never told me I was beautiful."

That seemed to still be an issue for her or she wouldn't have mentioned it...as the main reason for seeking traditional therapy. But did the therapy heal or cure her after 30 years? Obviously not.

She could have resolved her feelings of "needing something she didn't get" once and for all if she had done what I suggested in this chapter.

She could have sat down, done the relaxation, then imagined for 15-20 minutes that she was that little girl again hearing her mother say...

"*Oh, Barbra...I love you. You are such a beautiful little girl. You're the prettiest little girl I have ever seen, I'm so glad you're my daughter*", etc., etc.

If she had done that every time she felt the pain of not getting what she wanted from her mother the pain would have lessened over time and would eventually have washed away...because she was finally getting what she had wanted from her mother.

And **Key #2** - the Subconscious does not know the difference between what's real and what you imagine to be real. In essence, what she would have done was to "rewrite history"...having in her Subconscious Mind what she wanted when she was that little girl.

But trying to resolve her hurt feelings on a conscious/intellectual level -- by dealing with her situation as an adult instead of healing "the little child" that's still hurting -- she continues to struggle with the issue...for 30 years.

It's All In The Mind – But Which One?

Problems occur outside of us and as adults we remember those events in our conscious minds. But we don't consciously remember them when they happen to us as young children and only have a Subconscious Mind.

At whatever age we experience problems, the effects they have on us – how we internalize them, the attitude we create from them, the judgments they prompt us to make about ourselves, how they sadden our emotions and make our lives difficult – take root in our Subconscious Mind.

My experience has shown me that if you try to resolve yourself of those effects on the conscious level as an adult – by coming to "understand them" intellectually -- it will take a very long time to let them go...if ever.

CHAPTER 11

Don't Water The Weeds

I was working a job during the 1990's that allowed me to work as much overtime as I wanted. I was working 6 days a week for about 11 hours each. It wasn't a job I loved, but I was glad to have the overtime because I needed the money. I was working there for about five years when one day the company said…

"No more overtime for anyone."

Boy, was I upset. I took a negative attitude toward it. I was more than disappointed. Angry wasn't the word to describe it. I thought I was going to have to find a part time job to make up for the lost wages.

My negative attitude continued for several days wearing me down, although I didn't notice it at the time. Then, it hit me like a ton of bricks. I thought…

"Hey, maybe I've been working this job and long hours too long now. Not being able to work overtime is going to give me more free time to start looking for another job, to pursue other avenues of employment, perhaps exploring some freelance opportunities doing something I really love."

Then, I started to feel happy about not being able to work overtime. I started to look forward to the future with eagerness. I was about to make a big change in my life...for the better.

What changed in that scenario…the external event, or my attitude? The external event didn't change…"No more overtime" was still the new rule. Only my attitude toward it changed.

It's hard for many people to understand that *external* events have no effect on us. No matter how serious, catastrophic, depressing or tragic such an event can be in your life, the only thing that affects you is the attitude you choose to take toward the event. And we do choose our attitudes.

Beyond Positive Thinking

I know you've heard it before, that having a positive attitude is important... "*blah, blah, blah*"... and all of that. But because it impacts *everything* you do and *everything* that happens to you, we're going to take the topic to another level.

In fact, I'm not going to refer to it as a positive "attitude" anymore. I'll use the term "Positive Person". I'm talking about creating a positive mind, body and spirit. You're going to make your entire being positive down to every fiber and cell of your body. You're going to "rev up" that Law of Attraction as I explained in the Introduction and Chapter 7 so it works continually on auto pilot. The Law won't be very effective if you use it for a specific goal while the rest of the time your life is filled with negativity.

A Perfect Metaphor

First of all, I chose the title of this chapter after coming upon an anonymous quote. I think it's very fitting for this topic. It goes…

"Your life is your garden, your thoughts are the seeds, if your life isn't awesome, you've been watering the weeds."

It all comes back to a very simple concept that's so true...fill your mind ("your garden") with positive thoughts ("seeds") and your life will be a positive one. If you fill it with negative thoughts ("weeds"), your life will be filled with negativity.

By doing the assignment at the end of this chapter and seeing just the slightest improvement in your life will be all you'll need to show you how important it is to make EVERYTHING in your life positive. It will also be another step in taking your Mind Power to the extreme.

Even if your life has been a pretty successful one – you consider yourself to be in the fourth group I listed in the Introduction as to whom this book is for – trying this assignment will help you see if you can make it an even better existence. Maybe you have some small pockets of negativity ("weeds") of which you weren't aware that have been keeping you from being ALL you could be. You may come to realize you have even more potential for greatness that haven't been awakened – or "watered" – as of yet.

So stick with me, okay? You'll love me for it later when we really drill down deeply into your Subconscious and you begin to use Your Power to get just about anything you want.

There's an old saying you may have heard:

"*Your attitude determines your altitude.*"

It's your attitude that determines how high up in life you'll go. Being a positive person will take you to greater heights than will being a negative one.

Here's another old saying:

"*Attitude is the mind's paint brush. It can color any situation.*"

Think about those who have suffered greatly from tragic events – for example, a serious accident that left them paralyzed – but they go on to have very successful lives. Or those born with severe physical handicaps that don't keep them from succeeding in life. It's because of their attitude. They could have given up on enjoying life, staying in bed, feeling sorry for themselves and never accomplishing anything after that.

Of course, it's normal to feel depressed due to a depressing event such as a death in the family. But after an acceptable grieving period, you can either allow the crisis to keep overwhelming you to the point that you can't function. Or you can turn the crisis into an event that challenges you and forces you to take a positive attitude so you can rise above it and grow from the experience.

Here's another old saying (I've cleaned it up a bit, but you know how it goes):

"*Stuff happens.*"

Always keep this in mind. "Stuff" – bad stuff as well as good stuff -- will always happen in your life. This is not a Eutopia we're living in where we get what we want all the time and things always work out the way we plan them.

The key to managing "bad stuff" is how you deal with it. And when you become a positive person to the point that it becomes a natural part of you, it will seem that "good stuff" happens more than "bad stuff".

Many religious and spiritual leaders say crises in our lives are events to test us. Do we allow them to overtake us, or do we rise above them and become a better, stronger person? In either case, it depends solely on the attitude we choose.

You *Can* Change Your Attitude

You have to learn how to make EVERYTHING in your life positive for you to reap all the rewards life has to offer. Making the commitment to change your attitude from negative to positive is the first step. The next step – as that well known sportswear commercial from back in the day said – "*Just Do It*". It takes a conscious effort to make that change.

But if you have spent many years being a negative person you have to work to undo all of that in order for positive things to enter your life.

Flip The Coin

Start off by viewing your attitude as a coin that you can flip from "heads to tails", or in this case from negative to positive.

When you have negative thoughts you can instantly dismiss them by "flipping" them to positive. But you have to make a conscious effort to flip them or they won't.

That becomes easier as you proceed with your Mind Power development. Recognizing when you have negative thoughts is the first step to changing them. Many people have spent their entire lives steeped in negativity that they may not even be aware of it. Instead of concentrating on what they want they habitually reinforce in their Subconscious Mind the opposite of what they desire.

They focus on what they think they can't have. If you notice that happening to you at times all you have to do is "flip the coin" and start thinking and talking positively by focusing on what you want...tricking the Subconscious into believing you have it NOW.

You won't be doing something you aren't doing already, or that is in any way tiresome. You'll just be doing it differently...speaking to yourself in positive terms.

So you must recognize negative thoughts, then make a conscious effort to flip the coin to their positive side.

Let's say you're having money problems and you're saying an affirmation every morning to attract wealth. If later on you start to worry about your money problems it will undo what you're trying to accomplish with the affirmation. Stop worrying and say the affirmation for a few minutes to get the negative thoughts and emotions about your money problems out of your mind. That's flipping the negative to positive.

But to make your life a positive one on a more consistent and deeper level you need go beyond just thinking positive thoughts...you have to conduct yourself in positive ways, surround yourself with positive things, and live in a positive manner. Over time, it will happen.

If at first you find it difficult to make the effort to change simply believe in "The Power of Believing"…or stronger yet, simply *know* that your attitude has changed for the better. Convince your Subconscious Mind of that. Then your Subconscious will believe it and will make the change happen. In time, your new way of thinking will run on autopilot. And this will be a big step in taking control of your destiny instead of hoping things go your way...or worrying that they won't.

The Luck Of The Positive

A researcher wrote in the British Newspaper "The Telegraph" of a study he conducted to see if unlucky people can learn to become lucky. He found that his subjects who had claimed to be lucky had the same traits.

And guess what the number one trait that all lucky people have according to this researcher. That's right...a POSITIVE ATTITUDE.

And guess what the number one trait of unlucky people is as this researcher discovered. Right again...a NEGATIVE ATTITUDE.

Are you starting to see just how much of your life really is determined by your thoughts, one of which is your attitude...that we really are a product of our thoughts? So doesn't it stand to reason that you can improve your life by improving your thoughts?

As New Thought author and creator of "The Master Key System" Charles Haanel said…

"By far the greatest discovery of all the centuries is the power of thought."

Are you getting excited yet about what you're learning? And keep this in mind...you're just at the beginning stage of learning the Mind Power process. Your Mind Power really is the solution to all of your dreams... your desires...and also -- as you'll be learning later on -- to resolving your problems.

Traits Of The Lucky

Here's another characteristic that the researcher found among his subjects. Aside from having a positive attitude, lucky people ALWAYS and INSTINCTIVELY find the good in bad situations, while subjects who claimed to be unlucky always focus on the bad.

For instance, during the study one of the lucky subjects fell down a flight of stairs and broke a leg. The researcher asked the subject…

"Do you still feel lucky?"

The subject said…

"Of course. I'm lucky I didn't break my neck."

That's the kind of attitude you must adopt if you are to make yours positive and work *for* you. Always look for the positives in negative situations. Instead of focusing on what you don't have such as a job you love or a lot money, focus on the good things you have. Until you find your dream job, be thankful you at least have a job and are putting food on the table. If your house is just OK, be glad you at least have a house. If you're married with children and things are OK with them, be glad for that. Always look for the positives in your life and *feel happy* when you focus on them. Over time this will help change your attitude...and most likely your luck and your life.

Another trait the researcher found is that lucky people always expect positive outcomes from situations they enter, while unlucky people always focus on potential negative outcomes.

He asked his unlucky subjects to adopt the traits of the lucky ones. After just one month, 80 percent of the unlucky subjects reported seeing a definite improvement in their lives and even became happier. One woman who had failed three times to get her driver's license before she entered the study - and admitted to worrying about failing - finally passed the test because she expected to pass it.

A Simple Concept: Change Your Thoughts, Change Your Life

Many psychiatrists and psychologists will tell you the biggest single issue that determines what your life will be like is your self image...what you think and feel about yourself.

To make your _life_ positive you have to make _everything_ in your life positive. Half-hearted efforts will only slow your progress, and possibly keep you from the end zone. Associate only with positive people. You'll have to avoid negative friends. They'll only keep you in a negative attitude. Be honest with them...

"Sorry dude...I dig you man but I'm trying to turn my life around and your negative vibes bring me down at times. So I can't chill with you anymore. Nothing personal. It's just I'm trying to break the negativity in my life."

That will help them understand and possibly leave you alone. It might even help them to start ending their negative ways. Maybe the two of you (or 3 or 4...whatever the number) can work together in this endeavor.

As you start to become that positive person and "The Law Of Attraction" starts to work for you, you'll begin to see the positive in everything. It will be another example of the incredible Mind Power you possess. You'll start treating others in a more positive manner. And people respond positively to those who treat them with positive vibes.

You'll also be better at dealing with negative situations or road blocks without getting overly mad, or upset or depressed about it. You'll be seeing and living life completely differently. You'll now love life.

Take this mission on knowing the end game is to put your positive life on autopilot. If not, your life will continue on as it has up until now. Simply because you're reading this book, I think I'm correct to believe that's not what you want.

Getting started may be the hardest part. Not starting is easy. But as hockey great Wayne Gretzky is quoted as saying…

"*100% of the shots you don't make never go in*"…

meaning…not giving it a try, or not taking a shot at it ensures that your life will never improve.

However, here's the good news. Once you do take a shot at improving your attitude, your effort and the changes they'll make to your life will have a snowballing effect.

If you have trouble getting started, just remember all the benefits you'll receive:

- Looking at life in a positive way
- Rising above challenges and adversities that before would have overwhelmed you. And seeing fewer roadblocks in life than you saw before
- Less stress

- Drawing more positive situations and people into your life
- Allowing you to finally love your life

You've learned what making EVERYTHING about you positive means to your life. It's another step in realizing the tremendous Mind Power you have waiting to help you get just about anything you want.

Your Assignment

Tomorrow – provided you've reached the goal you chose at the beginning -- commit yourself to being a positive person all day long. Then just do it. Keep reminding yourself. Make the conscious effort. You'll have to get in the habit of "flipping that coin to positive" when you notice you're about to come up with a negative thought.

So to help you with that, every morning for the next week take a good 5-10 minutes to do the relaxation I showed you in Chapter 6, and just keep thinking to yourself for a good 15-20 minutes that you're a positive person...that you always look at things in a positive manner if problems arise. Tell yourself that you always look for something positive in those situations.

You can say an affirmation such as...

"I only hold on to positive thoughts. I always see the positive in things. People always respond to me positively now that I'm a positive person. I give out positive vibes to people wherever I go and they all pick up on it. My positive being always bring me success, happiness, money, joy, positive people who love me and I love in return. Everything about me is positive down to the cellular level. All my cells radiate positive energy."

Try that for the next week. You'll be killing two birds with one stone... getting your Subconscious programmed to always be thinking of positive things and thereby making EVERYTHING in your life great, and you'll begin the process of learning how to harness your Mind Power for bigger and better things we'll be getting to later.

Give it a try and just see what happens. I've given you examples of how things in your life will change but don't expect anything at first. You'll notice if your new way of thinking is producing a life you never knew was possible.

So don't go around trying to find results of your efforts. Don't get into thinking...

"Has anything happened yet? Am I seeing results yet?"

Here's another saying...

"A watched pot never boils."

Just let the signs of your effort happen...on their own. You'll notice the signs of your changing life when they begin.

And if you notice your thoughts going negative later in the day you have to make a conscious effort to make them positive. Start to say lines from the affirmation you did that morning for a few minutes. Training your thoughts to "go positive" will go a long way towards changing your life permanently.

And keep it going until it runs on autopilot. Do the affirmation and keep the positive thoughts and *feelings* going all day long and see how many other things – many more successes – happen in your life without thinking about them.

Even if you've always thought you're a positive person most of your life, try this assignment to see if even better things happen for you. Plus, you'll be using Your Power to attract even greater success and life events in the future...some of which we'll discuss later.

CHAPTER 12

The One Second Mind Power

Just to remind you...with every affirmation suggestion I've given you the key to it working is to say it over and over for a good 15-20 minutes. This is what makes Mind Power a more powerful transformation tool than Positive Thinking which is conducted on a conscious level. I'm not downplaying the importance of thinking positively. But to bring about "mind blowing", extraordinary success to your life you have to program your Subconscious Mind.

And I've said previously that the more you use Your Power the easier it works. How would you like it to work as easily as possible, say...within one second...or just a few, saying a one-sentence affirmation just once and without having to do the relaxation, even without feeling the emotion you would feel if you had what you affirm? Wouldn't that be incredible? How about...awesome? Maybe even magical? Is that even possible?

Your Mind Power On Steroids

By accident, I discovered how to put My Power into "overdrive" so that now it works "super" easily. I spent one full day doing an affirmation. After sitting in a chair and doing the relaxation, I did a 15 minute session in the morning before work then kept saying the affirmation all day, up to around 9pm. I accomplished that by forcing myself to say it every second I could in between the times I had to speak to people at work and in between phone calls while telemarketing.

At first, it was a challenge to keep saying it all day. But by around 3 o'clock that afternoon, it felt as if it were on autopilot. I said it practically without having to think about it.

My goal was to get anti-depressant medication out of me, and I wanted to do so quickly. When I would stop taking the medication after being on it for about 6 months, it would take 6 weeks to get out of me. And as the last bit of it – those final few molecules – would leave my system, I would get a head cold. But the medication that always worked great in the past when I got a head cold wouldn't work so well. I later realized why.

The head cold was not caused by a virus but by my body's reaction to that last little bit of anti-depressant medication exiting my system. There weren't any virus germs for the medicine to kill.

On the evening that I did the all-day affirmation, I got a head cold. So I went to the store to get my cold medicine. Later that night I noticed it wasn't working so well. I thought…

"This cold medicine is working the same as it does when I get a cold from coming off anti-dep…"

Before I finished my thought…Bingo!!!

A light went off in my head. My all day affirmation worked. I got the anti-depressant medication out of me in one day. That's why I got a head cold and the medication didn't work so well.

I thought…

"Wow! Something that takes 6 weeks to get out of my system on its own got out of me in less than one day by saying all day long 'the anti-depressant medication is gone, it has left my system. Every last molecule is out of me.'"

*(**Caution**: I recommend you do **not** try to get anti-depressant or any other mood-altering medication out of you this way. If you're on such medication and want to stop taking it, ask your doctor how to wean yourself off of it. When I woke up the day after doing the all-day affirmation I was the most depressed I had ever been. I had crying spells and suicidal thoughts all day. I eventually realized that it was the speed in which the medication left my system that caused those emotions.)*

I didn't know ahead of time that spending all day doing an affirmation and having it work would "Supercharge My Mind Power Into Overdrive." Now My Power works very easily. Here are some examples.

Poison Ivy...But Itching No More

I mowed the lawn about 6 months after doing the all-day affirmation. In the very back there's a slight embankment covered with ivy...some of it Poison Ivy of which I was allergic. When I was a kid I could get an outbreak of it in early March just from it blowing in the wind.

It was the day before Memorial Day and later that afternoon we went to my brother-in-law's for a holiday cookout. By that time I had an outbreak on my neck and arms, and it was itching like crazy, and spreading. Everyone was asking...

"What's that on your neck?"

I sat down to watch a baseball game on television and I thought with Memorial Day coming the next day it would be Tuesday before I could get to my doctor to get a shot of penicillin (I hate that topical lotion) and I didn't think of going to the emergency room that day.

I thought the itching would drive me crazier. I was starting to get a little sleepy but before I dozed off I thought...

"Why not try My Power to get rid of it? I've got nothing to lose."

So I said just one time…

"That Poison Ivy is all out of me. It doesn't exist in me anymore."

Then I dozed off for about 15 minutes.

When I came to, I resumed watching the game. I had forgotten about saying the one-second affirmation.

But a few minutes later I noticed I wasn't itching. I touched the bumps that had broken out on my neck and arms and they continued to get smaller as the day went on.

When I woke up the next morning, the outbreak was completely gone. There was no sign of it on my neck or arms. There were no more bumps, redness or itching.

I thought…
"Wow. I didn't even do the relaxation. I said the affirmation just once, not over and over again, and it worked. I didn't even feel the happiness of it being eliminated as I said it to myself."

I was blown away.

The next time I mowed the lawn -- just before I got to the back where the Poison Ivy is -- I closed my eyes and said just once (without doing the relaxation or feeling any emotion)…

"I'm no longer allergic to Poison Ivy. My allergy to it is gone. I can touch Poison Ivy now and it doesn't affect me at all."

That was in 1998. As I'm writing this it's 2020. I haven't had another outbreak since.

I really think it was saying that affirmation all day long to rid myself of anti-depressant medication and having it work that kicked My Power into high gear.

Another Example

I had my cholesterol checked and it was 260. Any number over 200 is considered unhealthy. So my doctor gave me all the information about diet and exercise. He said to have my blood work done again in 6 weeks.

I didn't change my diet or exercise because I wanted to see if I could bring my cholesterol down by saying an affirmation just once.

Two hours before I had my blood drawn for the follow up doctor's appointment, I closed my eyes, I didn't do the relaxation, and I said just once...

"My cholesterol has dropped to its most healthful level."

When I went to my doctor's appointment, he said...

"Hey, great job in getting your cholesterol down. You're off to a good start."

It had dropped to 220.

I did say...

"My cholesterol has dropped to its most healthful level"...

during my one sentence affirmation, correct?

While 220 is still unhealthy, it dropped 40 points. But I said the affirmation just two hours before I had my blood drawn. Maybe if I had said it 3 or 4 hours before it would have continued to drop to a healthy level somewhere below 200 by the time my blood was drawn.

I didn't affirm "my cholesterol has dropped to 180" or any other healthy number below 200 because that would have been a finite term. ***Key #4 - The Subconscious Mind only thinks in infinite or absolute terms.***

A Cure For Hiccups?

Ask any number of people if there's a cure for hiccups and you'll get many different answers. Do a Google search and you'll find many suggestions as to how to stop them. But if there is one scientifically proven way I didn't see one listed.

But I've found a way that stops them for me everytime. Now when I get them I simply say…

"I no longer have the need to hiccup. The hiccups have stopped. The condition that was causing me to hiccup has gone away."

Just those 3 sentences one time. I'll hiccup once while saying them, and then the hiccups stop.

Stop The Pain

If something falls onto my foot or I accidentally bang my hand against something and it hurts, I close my eyes and say…

"The pain in my foot (or arm or wherever it is) *has gone away. I no longer feel any pain. The pain is all gone"…*

and the pain stops in about 10 seconds. I imagine it would take a much greater effort the more intense the pain is.

Stop The Bleeding

When I cut myself while shaving or preparing food for cooking or engaging in another activity that produces a MINOR cut -- one not severe enough to require stitches or a bandage – I say…

"My blood has coagulated and has stopped bleeding. All the bleeding from my finger (or wherever the cut is) *has stopped. I'm not bleeding any further."*

If I cut a finger, I'll put it in my mouth and say the affirmation...just for 5-6 seconds. Or if I cut myself somewhere else, perhaps on my leg or arm...I'll put my hand around it as if it were a tourniquet and say the affirmation...and that stops it within a few seconds.

If you've experienced those types of cuts – surface cuts or those a little deeper – they can bleed for quite a while until you can put a band aid on them.

I haven't experienced a more serious cut since I've been doing this, for example...on a cut that would need stitches. But perhaps it could slow the bleeding down until stitches could be applied.

Stop The Sneezing

Have you ever had one of those sneezing episodes that go on and on? I know what they're like. But when I get one I stop it with My Power.

I'll say something such as...

"The Light of Healing has gone into my nasal passages and has eliminated the condition that was causing the sneezes. I no longer have the need to sneeze. They have stopped."

Then I imagine "The Light of Healing" is going into and up my nose to eliminate that condition. Just about 5 seconds is all it takes. I may sneeze once after that but that's all.

That Ugly Wart Now Gone!

Here's something I tried several years after doing the day-long affirmation. I didn't say it just once because I thought it would require more effort. But I'll never know. I wish I had said it just once to see. But this is still somewhat mind-blowing.

I used to have a wart on my left forearm. One day at work I turned in my chair and my arm -- right where the wart was -- hit the edge of my desk. A little bit of blood seeped out. I decided it was time to do something about it.

I could have had it surgically removed which would have required a $20 co-pay to see my doctor. Then he would have given me a referral for another doctor to remove it which would have cost me some more money because of a deductible with my medical insurance.

So I decided to try an affirmation. I sat down the next morning before work, did the relaxation and said for 15 minutes (over and over again)…

"*The wart on my arm has dissolved away. It's no longer there. Look! I'm looking at my arm and I can't see the wart anymore. It's gone. It has dissolved away.*" (I imagined looking at my arm and seeing that the wart wasn't there anymore.) "*I can run my fingers over the spot and it feels smooth. I can't feel the wart because it's not there anymore.*"

Then I imagined the sensation of my finger tips feeling that the skin of my arm at that point was smooth without the wart.

The next day a scab in the shape of the wart had formed because the skin had dissolved exposing the blood. Then the scab dissolved just as any scab would. About 5 days later there was just a thin flap of it attached to my arm.

Later in the day I noticed it had dislodged itself and was sitting in the hair surrounding that spot.

A few days later the spot where the wart used to be was completely healed, and now there's no sign of the wart. And all it took was five minutes of relaxation, and one 15-minute affirmation session.

Super Charge Your Mind Power

After you reach the goal you chose at the beginning of the book, try to kick start Your Power into high gear by doing a day-long affirmation. You'll have to constantly remind yourself to keep saying it.

Keep in mind that I had been using My Power for several years before I used it to get anti-depressant medication out of me in one day. Maybe that was all I needed to put My Power into high gear. And it still works as easily if I don't use it for several months.

In your first attempt at kicking Your Power into overdrive, don't get discouraged if you don't see results after one day. You might have to do it for several days.

Try it on something you can see. Or something internal such as pain... for example, from a sprained ankle or a sore muscle and you can feel the pain is gone. The key is trying it on something that you can definitely tell by the next day that you've accomplished what you affirmed.

I received an email from a salesman asking me if he could do the all-day affirmation claiming that he was the best salesman in the world. I wrote to him asking...

"How would you know that night or the next day that you've become the best salesman in the world? Try to affirm something that you can definitely tell that night or within a short time thereafter that it worked."

So he tried it on an allergy that caused a reaction from his sister's dog. He affirmed all day long that he no longer had the allergy. The next time he visited his sister, he had no allergic reaction to the dog. It worked.

Maybe you have a mole or birthmark or wart you'd like to get rid of. Do the affirmation...

"That mole (or birthmark or wart) *is completely gone."*

Say it all day long. Keep telling yourself to. Try not to look at it throughout the day to see if it's going away. That could reinforce in your Subconscious Mind that it's still there. Try not to look at it until the next morning.

But throughout the day, ***imagine*** you're looking for it but can't see it because "it's gone". ***Imagine*** while you're saying the affirmation that you're running your fingers over it and imagine the sensation of it not being there.

I suggest you don't try it for a head cold unless you start it at the very beginning signs of one and say it all day long. I've almost gotten rid of a head cold using my Mind Power but it took a tremendous amount of effort…three or four 15 minute affirmation sessions a day for 4 or 5 days.

And that didn't get it all. I had to use cold medicine to clear it completely. I probably needed to say the affirmation all day long to totally knock it out. I guess that's why there are no cures for the common cold. They're strong little "buggers".

Now when I feel a head cold coming on – I notice my nose is a little runny and I've had to blow it 4 or 5 times – I say…

"The virus that was making my nose runny has left my system. It's no longer in me. Every last molecule of the virus is gone now."

And that's all I say. By catching it early – before it reaches full blown status -- that stops it. Within several minutes my nose stops running. I might have to blow it just several times throughout the rest of the day. But when I wake up the next morning, there's no more runny nose or need to blow it.

Another Common Belief Shattered

OK kiddo...so you've learned from gurus NOT to say the name of a disease when trying to cure it because...

"you're focusing on something negative."

Here's the explanation you've been waiting for. In earlier chapters when I explained how to cure yourself of disease such as cancer, I said to say the name of the disease while using your Mind Power to imagine you're cured...

"The Light of Healing is shining like a laser beam on that tumor and has destroyed it."

Many gurus would instruct you to affirm something such as...

"I'm so happy to be cured." Or... "thank you for my healing"...

without saying the name of the disease.

It's OK to affirm things like that. But I also want you to say the name of the disease throughout the affirmation because if anything, your healing could happen much quicker.

When you affirm...

"The Light of Healing is shining on that cancerous tumor in my brain and has dissolved it away"...

you're NOT focusing on the cancer. You're focusing on the idea of *<u>not having it anymore, that it's gone.</u>* Plus, you're also feeling happy about being cured of cancer. Your happy emotions will have a bigger, positive impact on your Subconscious Mind than will the name of the disease.

Saying the name is not going to prevent the disease from leaving the body or cause it to do more damage than it would if you didn't say it.

I think I proved my point when I got poison ivy out of me, lowered my cholesterol and the salesman earlier in this chapter eliminated the allergy to his sister's dog. We said the name of what we wanted to eliminate.

And when I dissolved the wart from my arm, I affirmed...

"The Light of Healing is shining right on that wart on my arm and has dissolved it away."

And it dissolved away…because I wasn't focusing on the wart. I was focusing on it <u>not being there anymore...that it was gone.</u> Plus, I was feeling happy and relieved that it had dissolved away.

After sharing that experience with someone, I always ask…

"Now why wouldn't that work on a cancerous tumor?"

Everyone responds the same way…

"Well, cancer is more serious than a wart."

A flesh-colored wart is usually benign. But if I had struck mine hard enough against the desk tearing it off it could have become infected had I not gotten it quickly bandaged.

But that's not the point, whether or not a wart is less serious than a cancerous tumor. Is there anything positive about a wart…even if it poses no health threat of any kind?

If I do an affirmation to get rid of a tumor and mention it by name my Subconscious Mind is not going to think...

"Hey wait a minute. You want me to get rid of a tumor? Wow. I dissolved the wart for you and got Poison Ivy out of you and lowered your cholesterol. Those things are easy, but cancer is more serious. I don't know if I can do that."

I counseled a woman who wanted to get out of debt. I told her to affirm…

"I'm so glad I'm out of debt."

She said another Mind Power specialist told her to not to say the word "debt" because of its negative meaning.

I told her that by doing the affirmation as I suggested she would NOT be focusing on debt....she'd be focusing on being...*out of debt*... that she would be feeling happy about having all her debts paid.

The *feeling* of being debt free is going to have a bigger positive impact on the Subconscious Mind than the negative impact the word "debt" would have without any emotion behind it.

Saying the name of the disease or anything you're trying to eliminate while you're imagining it's no longer there will cause the Subconscious Mind to focus on it and destroy it...as long as you're feeling happy about being cured instead of worrying that you still have it.

END OF STORY, KIDDO!

PART 3

Beyond The Earthplane

CHAPTER 13

Space Is The Place

I received an email from a gentleman who had been studying my Mind Power lessons he signed up for at a previous website of mine.

He said one of his sons had been doing poorly in school for quite a while...scoring 30 to 40 out of 100 on all his tests. For 3 months he said daily affirmations stating his son was intelligent and was doing extremely well in school.

He never told his son he was using his Mind Power. And his son did not change his study habits.

When his son got his next set of grades 3 months later, he had scored 70 to 75 on all of them except for one in which he scored just below 50. The gentleman said he started to cry from the joy of his son doing better in school.

The father's positive affirmations – his thoughts – influenced his son without his son perceiving them on a conscious level. His improvement came about because we all have the same Spirit which makes all of us and everything else in the Universe interconnected..."The Law of Divine Oneness".

Although that example may not be proof "beyond a reasonable doubt" as scientists would claim saying "more studies are needed" (although it's proof enough for me), it's an example of at least a theoretical reason why our thoughts travel far and wide and can influence outcomes for whom your affirmations are directed.

Take Your Power Higher And Higher

So now, I want to take what you've learned so far to another level. Using your Mind Power to have a successful career and personal life – while certainly a great message and a great goal for which to strive – is a little picture. I want to show you a much bigger one and show you how you fit into this vast arena in which we live called "The Universe".

For now, set aside any doubts you have about this topic because when you "get it" and apply it a whole new world will open for you. Your Mind Power capacity will go far beyond anything you've realized so far. If you don't want to believe it, that's fine. You'll still be able to harness Your Power...but to a limited degree.

Your thoughts – even when you keep them to yourself -- are transmitted throughout the entire Universe and can affect any number of us. We don't have to consciously hear them as we do all the sounds we hear in our daily lives. We perceive them on a much different level.

A Mere "Speck Of Sand"

You may have already thought of this yourself, that each of us is a very small part of a Cosmic Whole which is the Creator of everything in the Universe. It goes by various names. Some obviously refer to it as God or the Divine. Others call it The Universal Subconscious Mind, Universal Consciousness, or Cosmic Power. But whatever it's called, I want you to understand that your Subconscious Mind doesn't belong to just you... it belongs to ***<u>EVERYONE!</u>***

Being a part of this Universal Subconscious Mind our thoughts are connected to this "Cosmic Power", and we can therefore communicate our thoughts and desires to it. Since it's the Ultimate Creator of everything in existence, it's able to receive your desires and make them a reality when you state affirmations correctly for whatever you're seeking...a better job, wealth, curing yourself of disease, etc. You're placing an order for something within the Universe and it's delivered to you. But who or what receives the order and delivers it?

Unfortunately -- to a certain extent -- science prevents us from overcoming our doubts about universal communication and just about any other concept that originates from within our Subconscious Mind... our Spirit. Science relies on theories being logically proved before it accepts them...and Science will never accept something that's illogical.

As I mentioned in **Key #6** our Subconscious is our il-logical, ir-rational, non-analytical, non-judgmental mind. So you can't make logical sense out of something that's illogical.

That's one reason why it's not unusual for many people to "pooh-pooh" what I'm talking about...perhaps even you are doubting it right now. But you don't have to believe it to harness your Mind Power to get just about anything you want. As I've said previously, you can be Atheist, believe that all I'm telling you now is baloney and still harness Your Power.

Yeah Todd, But Where's The Proof?

There you go again kiddo, trying to make *logical* sense out of something that's *illogical.* If the example at the beginning of this chapter didn't convince you there's plenty of anecdotal evidence of humans having telepathic abilities...being able to transmit information from one person's mind to another. Maybe those with the ability to do so are in the minority.

Or could it be that we all have this power but most of us aren't sufficiently aware of it to try and master it just as you're attempting to master your

Subconscious Mind Power? If you've never heard of telepathy – or have but don't believe in it -- you certainly won't master it if you don't give it a try.

But remember in Chapter 7 when I talked about using your Mind Power to attract your dream car (a Corvette)? I said one way it could happen would be by getting a promotion and a raise at your job giving you the means to get the car.

I also said this…

"If that's how it happens you could rationalize it -- and believe less in Your Power -- by saying…'He/she (your colleague) *got a new job and that allowed me to afford the car by getting that promotion. I didn't have anything to do with it.'"*

"Ahhhh, could it be that by using your Mind Power you influenced the boss' decision at the other company -- without him/her knowing it – to hire your colleague making their position available, and you also influenced your boss' decision to promote you and not another colleague without him/her consciously knowing it? I'll explain this aspect later."

The Universal Connection

Energy is more than the capacity to perform physical or strenuous activities. One of its definitions in the Merriam-Webster dictionary is...

"a usually positive spiritual force, the energy flowing through all people."

We don't see this energy but it connects us to each other and to everything else in the Universe.

Why are you attracted to certain people? Why do you "hit it off" with some people when you first meet? You can point to certain things that are consciously tangible, that you can "put your finger on" such as... "he's funny", or "she has a great personality".

Did he say to you..."hey, I'm funny"? Did she say..."hey, I have a great personality"?

No. So why did you come to those conclusions about them? You picked up on their aura, their "vibes"...their "energy". You connected with them on a Subconscious level. And therefore, our ***unspoken*** thoughts – which are energy themselves -- can and do influence others.

Power Beyond The Boundaries

You may have heard of or read accounts of people using their Mind Power to heal others of disease...even those who were thousands of miles away...even people who the healer didn't know, was made aware of them when their family members or friends asked the healer for help and showed the healer the person's picture.

So try that sometime. If a relative or close friend is ill, "Pray" for them... the correct way as I showed you in Chapter 9:

"*Oh God, thank you for healing* (name) *and curing her/him of* (name of disease). *I'm so happy that* (name) *is well now. Thank you Dear God. It is such a great feeling to know that* (name) *is completely healed. It was because you shined your Light of Healing onto* (name) *that healed her/him.*"

And feel the emotions you would feel if they were actually cured. If you're an Atheist/Agnostic leave out any reference to God:

"*Oh I'm so happy that* (name) *is well now. It is such a great feeling to know that* (name) *is completely healed. It was great to see him/her today and to see him/her full of life*" (then picture the person happy, full of life…just imagine it…and feel happy, just as you would if they actually were healed).

This brings me to what I mentioned in the lesson that talked about using your Mind Power to attract a soul mate. What if you've found yours but s/he doesn't love you?

Use your Mind Power. Do affirmations expressing thanks that s/he now loves you. Imagine the two of you together telling each other that you love one another. Imagine the two of you being together in exactly the way you want it to be.

Give that a try and see if s/he eventually loves you. For it to work it will take some time and daily effort…a good 15-20 minutes of affirming everyday that you and s/he are now together as one…and NEVER doubting it until it happens.

You accomplish things such as this with the help of three simple words… practice, practice, practice. Take your Mind Power to the extreme by practicing for extreme results...such as the following example.

Power Greater Than Mother Nature?

In 2019 Democratic Presidential candidate and spiritual leader Marianne Williamson Tweeted this before a pending major hurricane:

"The Bahamas, Florida, Georgia and the Carolinas...may all be in our prayers now. Millions of us seeing Dorian turn away from land is not a wacky idea; it is a creative use of the power of the mind. Two minutes of prayer, visualization, meditation for those in the way of the storm."

The media blasted her, claiming she was a wacko. She then deleted the Tweet and replaced it with this one:

"Prayers for the people of the Bahamas, Florida, Georgia and the Carolinas. May the peace of God be upon them and their hearts be comforted as they endure the storm."

She was right that her first Tweet was not a wacky idea. It was wacky only to those who haven't taken the time to learn what you have.

Taking On Sandy

In 2012 Hurricane Sandy was making its way up the east coast. Until this one, the area where I live was never ground zero for a hurricane in my lifetime. So I used my Mind Power.

For 15 minutes every day for a week leading up to Sandy's landing I affirmed:

"Thank you God for taking Sandy off shore and moving it out to sea. Thank you for keeping everyone safe. No property was destroyed and all lives were saved."

It didn't work out quite that way but my area was spared severe damage. Weather officials said if the storm had made landfall just 50 miles closer to where it was expected to my area would have been hammered. Many people would have died. Thousands of homes and businesses would have been destroyed.

But the storm continued up the Eastern seaboard clobbering northern New Jersey and Long Island. It was the fourth worst storm in U.S. history. Seventy two people died as a direct result, it caused $70.2 billion in economic damage, 650 thousand homes were damaged or destroyed, 8 million customers lost power, many for several weeks. People who had gasoline powered generators eventually ran out of fuel because gas stations didn't have power to run their pumps. Another 87 deaths occurred from hypothermia due to power outages, carbon monoxide, and accidents during cleanup.

So while the storm didn't go out to sea, at least my area – predicted to be Ground Zero – was spared. Was it because of my Mind Power? I'll never know. But I'll keep using it in times of pending disasters.

Mind Over A Deadly Matter

In January 2020 a new, deadly disease was sweeping across the Northern Hemisphere taking many lives and causing many businesses and schools to close.

In April I received a private message from a Facebook friend about a worldwide effort to stop it. It read:

"URGENT CALL FOR 1 MILLION MEDITATORS TO LIBERATE AND RECLAIM OUR WORLD ON APRIL 4, 2020 PRECISELY AT 10:45 PM EASTERN TIME WHEN A CELESTIAL STARGATE OPENS."

It was calling on people to use our minds to take the disease out of our solar system and the opportunity to do so – that Celestial Stargate opening at the precise moment of the Jupiter/Pluto conjunction – would last only 20 minutes that evening and the next day at various times throughout Europe, Asia and Australia.

I notified some friends and we took part affirming at 10:45 PM for 20 minutes...

"Thank you God for making that Celestial Stargate opening available to us. It has sucked the disease out of our solar system. It no longer is available to the world. Thousands of people have been spared."

The next day government leaders across the world announced that the rate of new cases and deaths was falling for the first time. The all important "bending of the curve downward" had begun.

So was our Mind Power the reason? We can never be sure. Many people would deny the idea by trying to make logical/rational sense of it and say...

"Well, the bending of the curve downward started a few days before that effort and it took several days to be revealed in the numbers."

Or...

"It was going to happen anyway. It just happened at the time of that world wide effort. The timing was just a coincidence."

Even if in reality it wasn't because of our effort, believing that it was keeps our Mind Power strong, making it even stronger. Doubting that our minds was the reason weakens our power.

So use Your Power often and stretch it beyond your conscious or logical limitations into the outer expansions of the Universe. Never doubt your power's abilities even to the slightest degree. It's limited only by how limited you think it is.

CHAPTER 14

Are You..."Programmed To Fail?"

Okay. The first 13 chapters dealt with learning how to harness your Mind Power to get just about anything you want.

Now, we've come to what I told you is what I believe separates me from the established gurus. Every one of them that I have read and/or heard speak in every self improvement modality from Self Empowerment/ Personal Transformation/The Law of Attraction, etc. says...

"Anyone can do this." Or...*"We all have the power to program our minds to give us what we want."* Or...*"This will work for everyone."*

But the real answer is…

NO! This will *NOT* work for everyone!

I said in Chapter 2 that it's what's in your Subconscious Mind – not your conscious mind – that determines what your life will be like. I also said this:

"If you read self help books or attend success seminars that show you how to set goals and you spend each day trying to attain them and you eventually have a great life, it's true that it was your conscious effort and desire to succeed that led you there. ***But the bigger picture is, there was nothing in your Subconscious Mind that stopped you (I'll explain this aspect later on)."***

Well, here we are at that "later on" point and it's time for me to show you "The Bigger Picture".

As I mentioned in the Introduction, a very common experience among those who have tried to use their Mind Power or any other Self Empowerment method to improve their lives is that it worked for a while, then STOPPED...and their lives returned to the way they were before they started. And further attempts to attain success failed. Has that ever happened to you? It's happened to me as I explained in the Introduction.

Why You're Struggling

If your life hasn't been what you've consciously wanted it to be this will help you understand why.

As I said in Chapter 2, no rational, sane person ever existed on this planet who *CONSCIOUSLY* wanted to fail and struggle through life. So if you're programmed to fail, the programming happened before your conscious mind developed -- generally speaking -- before the age of 4 or 5.

Here's one example. If your parents were always telling you…

"You're pathetic", or... *"You're stupid"*, or... *"You're worthless"*...

or other similar negative statements to the point you actually believed them, you could have developed low self-esteem, making you ***feel*** as though you didn't deserve to have anything you wanted if your own parents didn't think much of you.

At such an early age you weren't able to rationalize those feelings because you didn't have a conscious mind yet. But the negative judgments you made about yourself are still in your Subconscious. You programmed your Subconscious Mind through your emotions, which are just as strong at that age as they ever are.

If you've had a difficult life -- perhaps it seems you can never get what you want, as if something always sabotages your efforts to succeed at anything – you may think at times that something is punishing you.

But your Subconscious Mind never punishes you. It always protects you. If it believes by your thoughts and feelings from early childhood that you don't deserve anything because of your low self-esteem or whatever reason, it will prevent – or "protect" -- you from getting what you want later in life. You don't ***feel*** you deserve anything, even if you don't think that in your conscious mind...but that's what your Subconscious believes. It will see to it you don't get what you want. If it believes positively, that you DO deserve what you want, it will see to it that you get it. In both cases the Subconscious Mind worked the same way.

As you grow older and start to get conscious desires for things that any sane, rational person wants -- such as success -- your Subconscious will "protect" you from getting them because your original programming of not deserving what you want is still in your Subconscious Mind, which only thinks in the present **(Key #1)**. That program of not deserving what you want will always *PRESENTLY* be with you -- regardless of how old you get – until you change it with positive thoughts about yourself.

Real Life Example

I saw "Biography" on television when it was about Lee Harvey Oswald, who is believed to have assassinated President John Kennedy. Oswald's brother was interviewed and said their mother let them know in no uncertain terms that she considered her two sons to be burdens, not blessings. She did not love her kids...or at least did not show them any.

He said while growing up – even though Lee never said so out loud – he could tell that Lee was determined to prove that he was somebody. That was because in his Subconscious Mind, the feeling of being unloved gave him the self image that he was a "nobody"...had no sense of value if his own mother didn't love him.

So his emotional wound of not being loved started at an early age. And because it never healed, it *subconsciously* ate away at him driving him to make a name for himself.

The lack of love from his mother – plus being rejected by both the Russians and Cubans with whom he sought a partnership – made him subconsciously see himself as a nobody. In his ir-rational *subconscious mind*, killing Kennedy made him "somebody".

Pre-natal Programming

But can negative programming start before a person's early childhood? Many psychiatrists and psychologists say we can start to form our self image while in the womb.

If a woman becomes pregnant by accident, she may not want the child. If she's strongly disappointed about being pregnant and thinks of the child as a burden instead of a blessing, the fetus will know that because our Subconscious Mind is with us at the point of conception receiving and interpreting stimuli.

It could feel angry about not being wanted and the resulting person can carry those angry feelings all through its life and could act on them by getting into a lot of fights, becoming a violent alcoholic or maybe getting into crime.

They'll take their anger out on other people. They won't consciously know that they're angry with their mother for not wanting them because they didn't have a conscious mind when the anger formed. But those angry feelings from the womb will always *PRESENTLY* be with them in their Subconscious Mind.

If a mother gives her *angry* baby up for adoption, all the love showered on the child by the adoptive parents – the people who really want the child – will not erase that anger.

Do you remember the case in South Carolina around the turn of this century in which a white separatist beat an African-American named James Byrd, then chained him to the back of his pickup truck and dragged him to his death? He said he did so because he hated black people.

That was not the cause of his anger. He was adopted and his adoptive parents were not hateful people. They didn't teach him his white separatist views. In his Subconscious Mind – unaware consciously of his feelings – he was angry with his biological mother for not wanting him, even if she loved him but gave him up because she felt it would be best for him to be raised by other parents.

Hating black people gave him an outlet for him to channel and vent his anger. Yes, he hates. But without consciously knowing it he hates his mother for not wanting him and was filled with rage that he had to release by taking it out on someone.

A Serial Killer's Story

During the span of one year in the 1970's, teenagers sitting in their cars in a "Lover's Lane" around Brooklyn, New York were shot. Six were killed, seven were wounded. The gunman was nicknamed "Son of Sam" and is currently in prison serving six life sentences.

In a TV interview many years later, the New York detective who was the first to interrogate the gunman when he was caught said he asked him why he did it.

He said the first thing out of gunman David Berkowitz's mouth was...

"*My mother put me up for adoption.*"

Instead of going into a building and shooting people at random he may have thought – in his ir-rational subconscious mind – that no one was going to have love if he couldn't have it from his mother. Lovers were his chosen victims.

Again – in all those examples -- the feeling of being unloved caused their Subconscious Minds to be filled with anger and a desire to harm others...to take their anger out on "something".

When it's in the news that someone with a gun enters a school or store and shoots and kills people, then kills themselves, many people wonder…

"Why do people do things like that? I don't understand."

I'm not justifying their actions…I'm only saying I understand it. Those people are emotionally hurting. They have subconscious feelings of being a nobody, of being isolated from the rest of society. They want to end their lives…but not without first proving to themselves and others that they are "somebody"…that they will be remembered.

That's certainly not rational…but again, our Subconscious Mind – where the "need" to kill people is, to take their anger out on somebody – doesn't think rationally. And it all started with a feeling at a very young age -- for some while in the womb -- of not being loved.

These are just a few examples of how someone *may* react to a negative upbringing. Everyone is different. Many people who have grown up unloved or with very dysfunctional parents or in poverty – many adopted – have gone on to great things. How someone reacts to a negative upbringing depends on their psychological makeup.

But it all comes back to what I said in Chapter 2…that your conscious mind has nothing to do with who you are as a person. It's the thoughts and feelings in a person's Subconscious that causes them to do great things...but also evil, horrible things to people while being completely sane. They know what they're doing is wrong. And for many – perhaps even most – it's not a case of mental illness, but emotional illness.

Psychological Problems Are In The Subconscious

Those in the examples above whose minds are filled with negative self images from years of hurtful comments from parents or others "in their circle" can turn their lives around by learning how to change their thoughts. But they first have to come to learn that we are a product of our thoughts, that what's causing their problems is their subconscious self image. They then must make the conscious effort to change those thoughts from negative to positive.

Those with more serious problems such as anger for being put up for adoption must come to learn the source of those feelings and then release it from their psyche.

One way would be to use their Mind Power by stating affirmations such as...

"I release all the anger I have for my mother for not wanting me . I forgive her for not loving me and for putting me up for adoption. I release all the anger that was in me for that"...

and doing that for a good 15-20 minutes so the anger drains from their psyche (**Key #3**...repetition, over and over). But they first have to learn what the cause of their anger is and unfortunately, most of them never do. They'll carry that anger for a lifetime. They certainly won't resolve it and let go of it by...

"coming to understand it on an intellectual level and working to control their anger."

Either with the help of someone or on their own, they need to be guided into their Subconscious Mind -- where the cause of their problem is -- so they can identify it and then release it.

"Pre" Pre-Natal Programming

But there's another group of people – of which I and millions of others are included...possibly you -- whose problems started long before their childhood years…even before they were in the womb. Their problems are issues from previous lives that have carried over to their current one.

"Oh no, he says we have past lives? He's one of those wackos?"

Here me out for a moment. If you've read any books on the topic of past lives, they usually start off by saying something such as…

"*While there is no concrete evidence or proof that we have lived past lives, nothing is more fascinating than exploring the topic.*"

Well, I have MY concrete proof. I know from my life experiences that we DO have past lives because it was my past life issues that caused all my problems in this life. That's what kept me from being the person and musician I knew I could have been. That's what had that "grip" around me that I talked about in the Introduction. That's why I was a born loser and was programmed to fail. That is what caused my Mind Power development to STOP after it worked for a few months when I was a musician. That is what caused my life to become more of a "Living Hell On Earth" the older I got…until I resolved it all.

And if that is the issue that you're dealing with you most likely don't know it consciously, but it's keeping you from being all you can be. That is what's keeping you from having the life you want…keeping you from being a winner in the game of life. That's why you were born to be a loser with bad luck following you and your life in constant turmoil. It's what I've been talking about since the Introduction...

"The Unwritten Universal Law"

And if you are a victim your life will always be what it is now no matter what or how you try to end your struggles...no matter how many self improvement methods you try. You first have to resolve that unfinished business from a previous life.

In fact, if you don't at least try to resolve your unfinished business from a past life, your current life will only get worse. And those issues will follow you into your next life making that one more difficult than this one.

Perhaps this will convince you that the Past Life concept is credible. I was not a super Religious or Spiritual person while growing up. I never had a natural calling to the Spiritual world...never had a natural curiosity about such things as Reincarnation, Astrology or having Psychic abilities. None of those things was a hobby of mine as they are for many people.

If I had been a student of it from my early life, you could say...

"*Well, it's easy for you to believe in past lives. You believe all that other hocus-pocus stuff.*"

I never read books back then about those topics or anything else about paranormal abilities or supernatural phenomena. I was just an average guy about those things. I thought pretty much what "mainstream, everyday common people" think...that all that stuff is a bunch of "hooey" but didn't give it much thought beyond that.

Still not convinced about having past lives? Maybe this will help you see it. As I said earlier, I tried EVERYTHING I could find to resolve my failure issue...self help books, paid $129 to learn Transcendental Meditation (which is a great exercise for relaxation and relieving stress but not for changing someone from a born loser to a winner in life), put my Mind Power into action only to see it stop working after several months. What caused it to STOP?

I attended several Chanting sessions thinking that might work, spent 18 years in and out of traditional therapy trying to uncover what was holding me back.

Nothing worked...until I was informed that my past life issues were the problem. And when I started to deal with that and resolved it all – 13 years later – my life finally improved. And beyond just a few months. Is there a connection there...or is it just me?

So that's why I ***know*** we live many lives...not ***believe*** we do. It's a Truth I have come to experience firsthand.

Is it possible that I'm the only human being who has lived past lives and can't speak for the rest of mankind? I doubt it.

So we ALL have lived past lives. And we ALL will live an infinite number more. And that goes for atheists.

The Number One Question

I know what you're thinking...

"If I've had past lives, why don't I consciously remember them?"

Excellent question. It's the first one most people ask.

In each life you've lived, you were a completely different person. You had a different body, different genetic makeup, chemistry, AND a different conscious mind.

You -- the person you are now with the body you have, the consciousness, genetic makeup and chemistry -- _You_ have never existed before and _You_ will never exist again.

But your Spirit has lived many lives and will live an infinite number more. The only thing that's the same about you in every life is your Spirit. And I've never read this anywhere and no one has told me this…I've come to learn that your Spirit ***is*** your Subconscious Mind...your Subconscious Mind ***is*** your Spirit. You don't have a Spirit AND a Subconscious Mind, they are one in the same.

When we die or transition from one life our body and consciousness from that life end…but our Spirit/Subconscious Mind continues on to its next existence. Only the Spirit/Subconscious Mind reincarnates. And it remembers everything that happened to you in all the lives it has lived.

Everything you experienced, every thought you had, every judgment you made about yourself and every emotion you felt in all the lives your Spirit has lived is stored in your Spirit/Subconscious Mind.

And your Spirit is God's Spirit. God/The Creator is infinite…no beginning and no end. So your Spirit/Subconscious Mind is infinite. This is why **(Key #4)** your Subconscious Mind only thinks in infinite or absolute terms. Something that's infinite doesn't think in finite terms.

But your conscious mind is finite. It has a beginning and an end. The conscious mind you have in each life starts and ends in that life so you can't have any conscious memories of your past lives. (Some people do. But they're not the ones for whom I'm explaining this.)

When you transition from this life, your body and the conscious mind you have now will end. In your next life you'll be a different person with a different body, conscious mind, genetic makeup and chemistry with -- most likely -- no conscious memories of this or any other life.

But memories of *EVERYTHING* you experienced in all of your lives and the emotions you felt about them will still be in your Spirit/Subconscious Mind. And negative judgments you made about yourself in previous lives have carried over into your current life keeping you from being all you can be.

So now I'll ask the same question I posed at the beginning of this chapter and used as the title of this book:

Are You "Programmed To Fail?"

If you have reached the goal you chose at the beginning of the book… and all the "side effects" of positive affirmations I talked about earlier never stop and your life continues to improve then I would say…

"Congratulations. You are not programmed to fail because of unfinished business from a previous life."

If that's what happens, I'll be extremely happy for you. I'll be so thrilled that I helped show you the way. Not only have you reached your goal, you have learned how the Subconscious Mind works and you'll be able to use it to get just about anything you want. Just write a proper affirmation that states you NOW have what you want and put it to use.

So here's why I didn't want you to proceed with any of the Mind Power examples I showed you in Chapter 7 and afterwards until you accomplished the goal you chose for yourself. Or until after you saw your Mind Power efforts STOP a few months after they started to work.

If the affirmation you formulated to achieve the goal you selected has been working and things have been going your way and you see signs that you're attaining what you want and it continues that way for another 4 or 5 months and your life keeps getting better...great. You're not a victim of…

"The Unwritten Universal Law"

You're now an expert in Mind Power. You know more about it than most people ever will. After you reach your goal put your Mind Power to use in other aspects of your life...all aspects. Try some of the other examples I gave you in Chapter 7 and beyond. Then broaden your Mind Power arsenal by investigating other modalities, some of which I'll talk about next chapter.

What you've learned is just the beginning of your Mind Power Journey. There's an entire other world that's infinitely more vast than "this" one. And you've *always* been living in it without consciously knowing it.

It's a world beyond your conscious awareness that you can learn to tap into to lead you to greater greatness. This chapter was your introduction to it. I'll expand on it next chapter.

But...If You're A Born Loser Like I Was

However, if you were making progress in developing your Mind Power to reach your most important goal in life but it stopped working after several months and you feel your life is back to square one, then answer the following questions:

- Do you see yourself as a loser?
- Does it seem that your life is in constant turmoil?
- Does it seem as though you can never get anything you want... anything of a major importance?
- Or when you do, does something always take it away from you?
- Or if you are able to hold on to it, does it cause unintended or unforeseen negative consequences making the situation you wanted it for worse?
- Does it seem that bad luck always follows you?

- Do you have very few friends and/or think most people don't like you…even when you like people and want to be around them?
- Do you struggle with money even if you have a full time job most of the time, even in an industry that pays rather well?
- Can you never get a job and/or the romantic partner you really want?
- Have you tried to program your mind for success only to see it work for a while then stop, causing your life to revert back to the way it was before?

If you answered "Yes" to most of those questions – and definitely the last one -- I would say there's a good chance you're dealing with unresolved past life conflicts. And that means you are a victim of...

"The Unwritten Universal Law"

But don't get discouraged. Be happy and relieved you've found out that you're programmed to fail because of your past lives. Now you know why your life has been so difficult. You've taken a big step – a monumental one -- in your self-realization and now you know what you MUST do first before anything will improve your life.

For now you can forget about "The Law of Attraction", or "Mind Power", or any self improvement method because none of those things will help you...until you resolve your past life conflicts. Once you do, THEN those methods will work for you.

Most people who are programmed to fail because of unfinished business from a previous life don't know that that's the reason they're struggling and never will…in their current lives, that is. They've accepted their lives of failure, bad luck, constant disappointments and turmoil as simply fate and assume that it's just the way things will always be for them.

When things don't go their way, they'll say…

"Well, that's just the story of my life"...

and accept each failure and disappointment as reinforcement of what they've thought of themselves for many years…***that they're losers***.

But just as I was able to end my past life struggles, so can you. In fact, you MUST do something about it…NOW! I'll tell you what that is next.

CHAPTER 15

The Journey You Never Knew You're Taking

If you come to realize you're programmed to fail because of unresolved past life conflicts, I'll address your situation at the end of this chapter.

But if you've attained your goal by now or will soon and your life continues to improve…I'm extremely happy for you. It shows you're not programmed to fail and you'll be able to use your Mind Power to get just about anything you want.

So now, I want to encourage you to take your Mind Power to greater heights beyond what I've shown you so far.

In Chapter 9…

Let Us Pray...But Not That Way

I said you can be an Atheist and still harness your Mind Power. But in the previous chapter I said I was going to show you a whole other world that you're living in of which you may not be consciously aware. Even if you don't believe in a Higher Power, you are living in The Spiritual World.

Again, if you don't want to believe any of this that's fine. But please allow me to introduce you to the Spiritual journey that you're on even without you knowing or believing it.

Believe me. You ARE on a Spiritual Journey – in your Subconscious Mind, which I said in the previous chapter *IS* your Spirit. I'm simply asking that you allow me to make you *consciously* aware of it. It's up to you to decide if you want to jump on board so you can take your Mind Power to levels I haven't shown you yet.

I introduced you to this world in the previous chapter when I talked about the concept of your Spirit living previous lives. Now, I want to enlighten you further. I won't preach. I'll just explain.

Religion VS Spirituality

When I'm asked if I'm religious, I say…

"*No. I'm Spiritual.*"

Spirituality is different from Religion. I am in no way speaking negatively about traditional Bible-based Religion. It has been a tremendous help to many millions of people. I'm only explaining the differences between Religion and Spirituality as I have come to see them.

I think one thing that turns some people off from Religion is that they see it as a set of doctrines telling them how to live.

"*Don't do this, don't do that, don't do…*" whatever.

They see it as being too restrictive…having to give up a lot of what they see as "fun" in order to live a righteous life.

As I see it, Spirituality has no set of doctrines. It allows people to follow their own path in seeking out The Truth…in trying to find a Oneness with the Universe.

About the only obstacle to finding that Oneness that I can see is if one treats people in an Un-Godly way...physically harming them and/or their property, or by interfering in another's free will. One way to do that for example is to control and manipulate others, another is forcing others to do something they don't want to do. When it comes to Religious teachings though, I do have some trouble reconciling it all.

I was baptized and brought up in the Episcopal Church. Actor Robin Williams was Episcopalian. He called it "Catholic Lite". It's an order of Christianity that's the closest to Catholicism.

In church I was taught that God is a loving, forgiving God. But I was also taught that if we don't act the way He demands – if we sin – then we'll spend eternity in a burning Hell as our punishment.

As a young boy I had trouble understanding that. I saw it as inconsistent with the concept of God being loving and forgiving if he punishes us instead of forgives us for our sins.

Spirituality teaches that there is no sin. If we go against God's laws and treat others in an Un-Godly way, we make mistakes that need to be corrected. Our Spirits don't spend an eternity of punishment in Hell.

After we die or "transition" from each life, the Spirit returns to earth as a different person. When it chooses an incarnation to correct all the mistakes in how it treated people in previous lives and then does so, it can choose to then live its next incarnation in another galaxy -- free from all the perils we humans face here on earth – and get one step closer to the Oneness with the Universe that ALL Spirits are seeking. Thus, past lives and reincarnation of the Spirit. To me, that's more consistent with God being loving and forgiving.

Another religious teaching I had trouble understanding was the need for us to be "God-fearing". Does that mean we worship God and do what he says out of *fear* for what will happen to us if we don't? Hell, fire and brimstone? Or do we worship God and act like Him towards others out of *love* for God.

That's what Spirituality teaches...how to be God-loving towards others.

I've also come to see that Religion teaches a distinction between man and God...that we are God's creations, His subjects...that we are separate from God.

Spirituality teaches that we ARE God...we have the power of God within us because our Spirit is God's Spirit...that we are "little droplets of God", that therefore, we all have the same Spirit while still having our own unique personalities.

Here's another issue I had trouble understanding. God gave us the gift of free will. While he's instilled in us certain laws so we can live in civilized societies – don't harm anyone or their property, or steal from anyone, or force another to do anything against their will... laws we were all created instinctively knowing -- he gave us freedom to act as we choose, even to break those laws.

But to be eternally punished if we choose not to act the way He tells us to? That's not consistent with free will. It's as if God said...

"I love you so much I'm giving you the gift of free will. You're free to act any way you want. You're not created to live your lives only by instinct as animals are. But if you don't act the way I tell you to, I'll punish you by sending you to Hell for eternity."

That's not much of a choice.

Spirituality teaches that we do have freedom to choose whatever we want. If we act Un-Godly towards others over a number of incarnations – even commit murder -- God won't punish us. Our Spirit will decide it's time to change its ways and will choose one of its incarnations to correct those mistakes so it can learn from them...come to understand that what we did to others in previous lives was wrong.

And the only way it can come to see the wrongfulness of its ways is to choose a life in which it subjects itself to being treated as it wrongly treated others in previous lives. It chooses to "put the shoe on the other foot" so to speak. How else can it learn from the mistakes it made in previous lives than by choosing to be subjected to the same thing?

That's why people struggle in certain lifetimes by never getting what they want, bad luck always following them, their lives in constant turmoil… and thereby causing their mind power or any other self improvement modalities to STOP working after a few months causing their lives to return to the way they were before they began…***being a LOSER!*** They're a victim of…

"The Unwritten Universal Law"

Their Spirit has chosen an incarnation to live "Hell on Earth". When all those past life issues – called "Unfinished Business" – are resolved, ONLY then can that person have a happy life...the life they long for. ONLY then will their self improvement efforts produce life-long results.

In my experience, Spirituality gives me a much greater understanding of the powers and laws of the Universe (the "mysterious" I talked about in Chapter 2) and a greater sense of being connected to everyone and everything in the Universe than does traditional Bible-based Religion.

So that, my friend is just a brief introduction to the world of Spirituality through my eyes…the basics or the fundamentals so to speak. I could go on and on explaining it deeper and deeper. But it would be my vision of it. If you decide to *consciously* take part in your Spiritual Journey to use it to your advantage – to take your Mind Power to the stratosphere – you'll probably come to see those fundamentals as I explained them.

But the rest of the story – which is as never ending and as vast as the Universe itself – would most likely be realized through your interpretation and life experiences.

So What's This Have To Do With Mind Power, Todd?

Do you see yet how it's all connected? Your life is not determined by your conscious mind but by your Subconscious, which is your Spirit. You have a Spirit that's on a journey to learn and grow…to find that Oneness with the Universe…to become more God-like.

You do live in The Spiritual World, even if you don't believe it or know it consciously. It's as if your conscious life is here on Earth…"The Earth Plane". But your Spirit/Subconscious is living "out in the Universe" – beyond your conscious awareness -- while still being part of you.

Does that make logical sense? Of course not. Your Spirit/Subconscious Mind/God/The Creator Of Everything In The Universe/The Universal Subconscious Mind…all of that is il-logical/ir-rational **(Key #6).**

And the Spiritual world offers a huge arsenal of modalities that can take the Mind Power teachings you've learned from this book to even higher levels. I'll introduce you to just a few of them. Again, it's up to you to decide to investigate them. Just keep an open mind is all I ask.

Astrology - I'm talking *legitimate* Astrology not the horoscopes found in newspapers and magazines. Or websites in which you put in your birth date and get a reading in a few minutes, or the pop culture variety of it which you hear at the singles' bars a lot…

"Hi there, what's your sign?"

A true, legitimate Astrological reading involves more than just your sign and/or birth date. It also involves the time of day you were born and the location of your birth…the longitude and latitude of planet Earth. And it can take an Astrologist many hours to complete your "chart".

If you begin to investigate your Spiritual journey, you'll come to learn that while we're in Spirit form, we choose the time, date and place of our birth. Legitimate Astrology is a scientific study of how the alignment of the planets along with specific magnetic fields of the Universe at the time of our birth determine how our lives will be.

Before we're born our lives are pretty well mapped out according to this information. That's why we choose the time, date and location of our birth. How the elements of the Universe are aligned when you're born will ensure you have the life you chose for yourself while you were in Spirit form.

If you chose a life of struggling because your Spirit wants to resolve unfinished business from a previous life, legitimate Astrology will help you change your destiny by seeing into your Subconscious world – the part of you living "out in the Universe" – so you can determine the appropriate changes you must make to improve your life. That takes your Mind Power to another level.

Still think Astrology is a bunch of baloney? Have you had a *legitimate* Astrological reading with an expert? If not, then I urge you to be open-minded. Here's my experience with it.

I told you previously I was in and out of therapy for 18 years. At the conclusion of my first appointment with a new one he said…

"I think the solution to your problems is getting more into other people."

A few days later I called a friend of mine. I didn't know she was into Astrology as a hobby. She told me she had done my horoscope. I chuckled a little thinking – as you probably are – that Astrology is a bunch of nonsense. She said…

"Boy, you've really had a rough life haven't you? I think the solution to your problems is getting more into other people."

That floored me. It was exactly what the therapist told me. I shared that with him at my next appointment. Even he seemed a little stunned. He said...

"*She picked up on that just from your birth date?*"

When she did my horoscope she only knew of my birth date. From her I learned that for an accurate reading, legitimate Astrology also requires a subject's place and time of birth. She later did a full reading with all the necessary information then read me her findings. She had my life story "down to a T".

So please, just keep an open mind as you investigate these modalities. Experience them with experts, then decide. Or select one of them, study it and put it to use yourself...then decide.

Tarot Cards – If you've never heard of these cards, it's pronounced... TAR-o. The "A" is pronounced like the letter "a" in the word "at". By studying them you acquire another tool for taking your Mind Power to greater heights.

Tarot Cards can help you acquire information about your past, present and future. Understanding the patterns from the cards' images can help you learn what's going on in your Spirit/Subconscious Mind and what's likely to occur from that "beneath the surface" activity.

Tarot Card readings can help you understand the Spiritual world and the journey in which you're traveling. They can assist you in uncovering the reasons for unwanted negative patterns such as fears and phobias from past lives that you don't know where they came from and you can't eliminate. The Tarot can also help you make important decisions.

Akashic Records – I've heard this pronounced two ways..."ah KAH shick" and "ah KAY shick".

Your Subconscious is like a computer that stores all your thoughts, feelings, experiences and judgments you made about yourself in all your lives? Think of the Akashic Records as a Super Computer that has stored every thought, word spoken, experience, event, and emotion felt by EVERYONE who has ever existed in the history of the Universe.

Wow! What a data bank that is. The records connect EVERYONE and EVERYTHING that has ever existed...on this planet and beyond.

By learning how to read The Akashic Records you take your Mind Power to a greater level. You'll be able to hear thoughts and feel the emotions EVERYONE who has existed has had. That's what I mean in the Introduction when I said I'll show you how your thoughts travel far and wide within the Universe for an eternity. The Akashic Records stores them all there.

You can experience EVERY event that has occurred throughout the entire Universe. You can discover what you thought about yourself and events that happened to you in previous lives. That can help you uncover reasons for problems in this life that you haven't been able to resolve.

Pretty neat, huh? To say the least.

Numerology - Numbers, numbers, numbers! Everyday we're bombarded with numbers. We can't escape them...phone numbers, birth dates, financial information, license plates .... AGGGGHHHH!!!!!

Whoa! Relax, dude. Take it easy. Numbers provide another weapon in your Mind Power arsenal.

Numerology is the study of how numbers affect our lives. An expert takes a full name or a birth date and reduces it to a single number. With that number the expert can pick up on certain things about the subject's character, strengths, weaknesses and can even predict their future.

Each number from 0 to 9 has its own set of values. Many Astrologists rely on Numerology. They'll assign one of those numbers to each celestial body in the solar system in order to get a subject's accurate reading.

Numerology has been around for thousands of years and many people are learning how numbers can affect them.

(Have you ever wondered why the symbols for numbers are universal… even within languages that have their own alphabet such as Russian? Just a thought.)

Lucid Dreaming – This is the state of dreaming while being consciously aware that you <u>ARE</u> dreaming. Once you're aware you can change your dreams and control what happens in them. When mastered, Lucid Dreaming allows you to control the direction of your dreams.

You can dream that you've uncovered and released fears and phobias and other problems that are in your Subconscious Mind, causing those problems to vanish.

It works because your conscious mind is out of the way allowing you to solve problems creatively in a 3D environment. It also helps you expand your Mind Power as it helps you to draw deeper insights into your Subconscious Mind where most – if not all -- of your problems and strengths originate. You can then resolve the problems and capitalize on the strengths.

Develop Your Psychic Ability – Have you ever started to think about someone you hadn't talked to or even thought of in a long time – perhaps years -- then a short time later you got a phone call from them?

Have you had a problem you needed to solve – let's say an issue on your job – and you thought about it over and over but couldn't come up with the answer? Then one day when you weren't thinking about it the solution popped into your head "out of the blue?"

Have you ever had a dream that came true? Do you ever get "hunches" that turn out to be correct? All of those things are your Psychic abilities at work.

Any legitimate Psychic will tell you we are all Psychic...some people more than others. And you can develop those abilities and add further fire to your Mind Power simply by practicing.

Trust your hunches and act on them more. When your phone or door bell rings try to think of who it is before you answer. You may not have as much ability as those who were fully empowered with their gift at birth. But you can fully develop whatever ability you have. Practice these skills just as you've practiced to develop your Mind Power skills.

Still don't believe Psychics are legitimate? Did you know that police departments all over the world rely on them to help solve cases? They're called Paranormal Investigators. Police would not use them if they weren't credible.

Go to a legitimate Psychic (preferably one who doesn't advertise unless you personally know people they've helped) and they start saying things about you that they would have no way of knowing and it will really floor you.

So there's a list of just some of the many modalities in the Spiritual world that you can use to take your Mind Power to greater heights...to give you "Super, Super Mind Power" or maybe even..."Ultimate Mind Power". All of them do so by allowing you access to your Subconscious Mind where all your power is...along with about 99 percent of your being.

Now that you're an expert on how the Subconscious Mind works, you'll be able to harness the power from these and other modalities a lot faster than non-experts.

If you decide not to take a look at your Spiritual journey to investigate these and other modalities, that's fine. I just wanted to make you aware of them. Maybe you'll choose to take a look at them in your next incarnation.

If it all still seems like "hocus-pocus" I think I would be correct to say you've never had a reading from an expert. Or if you have the practitioner was not very good.

But if I've piqued your interest and you want to take a step into the "mysterious" and gain from all that the Spiritual world has to offer, a good place to start is by examining your past lives.

If your life has been a pretty good one so far you can make it even better. Check out my book, ***"Exploring Your Past Lives: The First Leg Of Your Spiritual Journey".*** https://www.amazon.com/Exploring-Your-Past-Lives-Spiritual/dp/B08DSND2MV/ref=sr_1_4?dchild=1&keywords=todd+wissler&qid=1596635641&s= books&sr=1-4

If you're dealing with fears or phobias you don't understand and can't resolve, or you have medical conditions in which treatments aren't helping, those issues could have carried over from a previous life. You could find some help in my book, "***Uncovering Your Past Lives: Freeing Yourself Of Unexplained Fears, Phobias, Traumas And Untreatable Medical Conditions".*** https://www.amazon.com/dp/B08F6TXRM8/ref=sr_1_7?dchild=1&keywords=todd+wissler&qid=1596635709&s=books&sr=1-7

Now, if you've practiced your affirmation and were getting results from it for a month or two and now the results have stopped and your life is back to what it was like before you started to read this book … there's only one reason for that. You're programmed to fail because of unfinished business that has carried over from a previous life.

You're now in the incarnation your Spirit has chosen to resolve the mistakes of treating people in Un-Godly ways during previous life times. Your Spirit wants to correct those mistakes so it can learn and grow from them so it can move up the ladder of Spirituality and become more God-like.

But before that can happen you must uncover what those mistakes were so you can correct them and rid the demons from your current life.

If you don't correct those mistakes in this incarnation the problems you're having will follow you into your next life making it even more difficult than this one.

To help you in this endeavor get a copy of my book:

"Resolving Past Life Issues: Breaking The Chains That Keep You Failing".
https://www.amazon.com/Resolving-Past-Life-Issues-Breaking/dp/B08DDS85MB/ref=sr_1_2?dchild=1&keywords=todd+wissler&qid=1596635768&s=books&sr=1-2

All three books are on Amazon. In each of the three scenarios I just mentioned, you'll be using a process called "Past Life Regression", or "PLR". If you want to learn more about it before you purchase any of my past life books, you can sign-up for my FREE e-book...

"Past Life Regression Basics - Who Were You Many Lifetimes Ago?".
which is available at my website. And while you're there be sure to sign up for my monthly Mind Power Lessons called "Success Exclusives":

www.SuccessExclusives.com/mind-power-lessons/

Once again, thank you for allowing me to help get you going on your Mind Power and Spiritual Journeys. I truly hope this book has helped you. I would love to hear about your experiences with it...and my desire is for you to have everything you want in life.

Bibliography

1. https://www.rogerebert.com/reviews/great-movie-the-color-purple-1985
2. ***"Attaining Satisfaction",*** by Cecile K. Cho and Gita Venkataramani Johar. Journal of Consumer Research; December 11, 2011
3. ***"Succeed: How We Can Reach Our Goals",*** by Heidi Grant Halvorson, Ph.D. Published by Hudson Street Press

www.ingramcontent.com/pod-product-compliance
Lightning Source LLC
Chambersburg PA
CBHW072019060426
42446CB00044B/2802

* 9 7 8 0 5 7 8 7 9 8 2 8 8 *